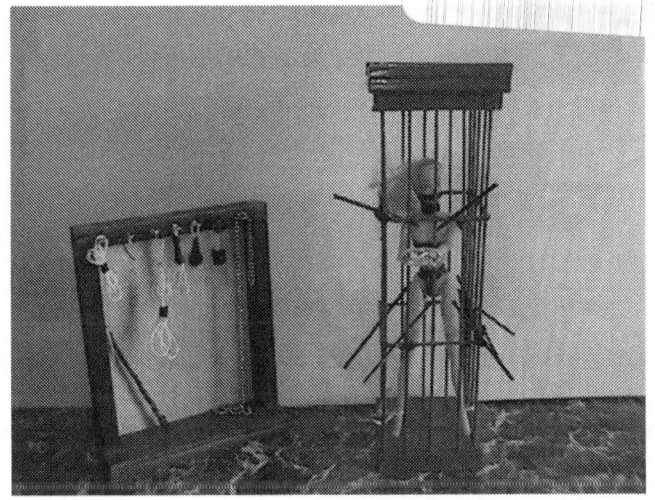

"Rema's Revenge"

By

"I. B. Cuffman"

"Rema's Revenge"

Copyright @ 2007

By

Rich B. Publishing

All rights reserved

No part of this book may be reproduced, stored in any retrieval system, or transmitted in any form without the written permission form the publisher and author.

Published in 2007

All depictions and characters are fictional, and over the age of 18. Any similarity to real persons, places, or things is purely coincidental.

Book design
By
Rich B. Publishing
P. O. Box 404
Nichols, South Carolina
29581

E-Mail--RichBPublishing@aol.com

Published in the United States

ISBN # 978-0-6151-7100-5

Introduction

A search of documents led Bryan from the hallowed ground of London to the picturesque beaches of South Florida to exotic Japan. His target was the kidnapper and gunrunner Tony Rema, who with his henchmen kidnapped numerous women and for profit. While Bryan was on his mission, his lovely Kim became the property of the sadistic Rema and was forced to serve his every sadistic wish, usually by a whip.

Rema had escaped capture in his submarine and was now on a voyage to deliver a shipment of illegal weapons to the North Korean Army and his latest client and assistant, Colonel Lee Suko. Sadistic violence, savage sex, and BDSM at its best follow Bryan on his trek from Madam Wong's pony girls to Mama Sandju's Pleasure Palace. It's only a matter of time before they meet to settle the score.

Table of Contents

Bryan's Mission	*Chapter 1*	*Page 1*
The Search	*Chapter 2*	*Page 17*
The Raid	*Chapter 3*	*Page 29*
Madam Wong's Estate	*Chapter 4*	*Page 45*
Kim's New Owner	*Chapter 5*	*Page 63*
The Chase	*Chapter 6*	*Page 75*
Janet's and Kim's Torment	*Chapter 7*	*Page 93*
The Stewardesses	*Chapter 8*	*Page 108*
Mama Sandju's Pleasure Palace	*Chapter 9*	*Page 120*
Suko's Dungeon	*Chapter 10*	*Page 135*
Operation Rema's Crew	*Chapter 11*	*Page 149*
Operation Suko Point	*Chapter 12*	*Page 158*

Bryan's Mission (Chapter 1)

Only a few months had passed since the ordeal with Ted Darling and the rescue of the kidnapped women from the *Colletta*. Bryan was glad that he could now settle down and put that mess behind him. With the money Bill had given him from the ship, he was able to purchase the house he wanted at Pikes Point. He loved the isolation the place offered: only one way in and one way out. The view overlooking the point, the rolling waves from the ocean, and the sandy beach were breathtaking.

Kim moved in with him almost immediately and helped him renovate the place. New furniture and lavish carpet in each room made the house comfortable, and the new workshop gave Bryan the chance to enjoy his woodworking hobby.

After the upstairs work was completed, they shifted their attention to their favorite room: the basement. Bryan had told Kim about his friend Nick Baxter from out West and his unusual method of decorating his dungeon basement.

They took special care in acquiring and arranging the special furniture they wanted: some things Bryan had to order, and some things he made himself in his workshop. Kim took special care in the construction of the spanking bench, the "X" frame and the stretching table. She figured she would be spending a lot of time tied to the equipment, so why not make it as comfortable as possible?

They spent a lot of time shopping for other special items. Whips, chains, and leather cuffs were high on the list of necessary items. There were two electric hoists that were secured to the basement wall, one on each side of the room. Each had long cables that hung from large pulleys in the ceiling. Metal bars were attached to the cables with eyebolts at the ends of the bars.

Bryan stepped back when the last touches were complete and appraised their efforts in the room; even he was impressed with the excellent opportunity for Kim's suspension.

"Kim, not bad, not bad at all," he told her, thinking back to his friend's basement. "Just like Nicks."

It was early Friday evening, and they were both eager to test some of the equipment. "Are you ready for a session on the spanking bench?" he asked, lightly paddling her bottom.

"Hell yes," Kim said, smiling as she looked up at him with sparkling, sexy dark eyes. "If I can handle what that bastard Rema did to me, then I can handle just about anything."

Bryan loved her eyes—they told so much about her enthusiasm to be his pleasure slave. "Well then," he said, waving his hand in the air, "get those clothes off! I get so damn excited when you're naked." The isolation of the house allowed them to be less restrictive about wearing clothes. Most of the time, Kim didn't wear much; Bryan liked that.

It only took a few seconds before she stood naked in front of him. Bryan admired the splendor of her ravishing beauty and her essence of womanhood. Her sumptuous smile radiated the majestic elegance of the girl next door. Her breasts were firm but soft at the same time; her hard nipples begged to be kissed and played with. He especially loved her rounded hips and her shaven pussy; with no hair it was easier to taste her fabulous nectar.

She watched him admiring her and was fascinated that he favored her body so much. Still standing there, she spread her long smooth legs a bit so he could get a better view of her exquisite slit. Bryan said nothing. Then Kim bowed her head and tossed her silky hair to one side as she moved to the padded bench and straddled it like a horse. With her knees on the bench's side-padded supports, she lay down on her stomach, causing her arms to fall beside the bench's front legs with her hands almost touching the floor.

Bryan tied her wrists and ankles to the legs of the bench with soft cotton rope. Her forehead pressed into the vinyl cushion at the head of the bench, causing her to arch her beautiful tight ass and pussy upwards. Her slip opened slowly for him to see and touch.

Bryan selected his favorite whip: a short-handled one with two leads and four poppers. Over the last several weeks, he had become very proficient with this whip. Kim had remarked on how much she liked the feel of the whip; it seemed to caress her skin.

He raised his arm and gave her ass a light stroke with the whip. The contact was not severe, but the slap echoed throughout the room. She wiggled her ass a little but restrained as she was, her position did not change.

The second stroke crossed her ass harder than the first, causing her to raise her head from the cushion. A small gasp of air escaped her parted lips. Her eyes closed as the third stroke landed with even more intensity.

"Aow!" she cried with the next stroke, twisting to one side, her hair flying in all directions. Small red lines marked her ass on both cheeks. She pushed her ass up and back challenging him to do more. Bryan could tell she needed to feel the sting; the compulsion was too great.

He stopped the whipping and moved around to face her. He gently put his hand under her chin and looked deeply into her soft sparkling eyes. The incredible expression of anticipation and desire he saw was that on an emotionally sex-driven woman.

"Are you okay?" he asked softly.

"Yes," she said in a soft obedient voice. "Yes, I'm fine. I cherish the whip. Please, sir!" she begged, "Don't stop, I know it will make me come. Please make me come." Beads of sweat started to toll down her cheek.

Even face down on the bench Bryan could reach under her and cup both of her breasts. He squeezed them at the same time. He kissed her lips and forced his tongue deep inside her mouth. Their tongues played with each other for some time. Finally, letting go of her breasts, he pinched each nipple.

"Oh! Oh! She cried softly, wincing from the pinch.

"You like it," he said. "I know you do." He moved back to her backside and lightly rubbed her ass cheeks with his hands. Again, she wiggled at his touch. "You don't want me to stop, do you?" he remarked.

"No sir! Please." She turned her head as far as she could toward him and licked her lips. "Please continue. I crave you to continue."

Bryan could see the delightfully eloquent glow on her face, but he was lost in his own delicious obsession of desire. "As you wish, my elegant slave," he answered. He made a few passes with the whip over her back, not touching her.

Feeling the air move against her skin, Kim dropped her head back to the cushion and closed her eyes again.

The next strokes were to her back and shoulders, lightly at first, then increasing in intensity. Bryan was toying with her, teasing her, bring her body to incredible highs of sensual emotion.

"*Ahee!*" she cried at the fervent burn of his next strokes, the whip lapping at her skin. He watched her struggle in her escape-proof bonds; the effect on him was intoxicating. He gave her several light strokes and then a vicious cut. "*Ahee!*" she screamed, her body dancing to the tune of the sadistic whip.

The skin on her back and ass was blazing red, crossed with scores of long scarlet stripes. Bryan could see it was an excellent burn; she had come at least twice, maybe even a third time. He laid the whip down on the floor next to her.

"I'll be back in a few minutes. You just wait here," he said jokingly. "I'll get us a beer. I think we both could use one."

Bryan had just opened the icebox door to get the beer when the telephone rang in the living room. He picked it up. "Hello! This is Bryan."

"Hello, Bryan. This is Greg Jeffers, do you remember me?"

"Yes, sir, I remember you. You're the regional director from the government. How could I forget that night? I was just glad we could stop those guys from taking those women. Have you been able to catch that guy Tony Rema and stop his gun-running?"

"Not yet, I'm afraid," Greg replied. "We haven't been able to locate the submarine yet; it may take us a while. In any case, I do need to talk to you. I'm here with Bill in his office. Is it possible we could meet in the morning around ten?"

"Yes, sir. I'll be there," he responded.

"Oh!" Greg remarked, then asked, "How's that lovely Kim these days?"

"Well, sir, I have to spank her ass with a whip once in a while to keep her straight, but she's doing fine," Bryan replied.

"Okay, then," Greg chuckled, "See you in the morning."

Bryan returned to the basement and untied Kim's wrists and ankles so she could sit up and drink the beer that he gave her.

"I heard the phone ring. Who was it?" she questioned, taking another swallow of cold beer.

"You remember Greg Jeffers, don't you?" he asked.

"Yes, I do." She looked puzzled. "What does he want? Did he say anything about Kelly and Peggy?"

"He didn't mention them, and I'm really not sure what he wants, except that he wants to meet with me around ten in the morning."

The next morning, Bryan escorted Kim to the basement, as he always did on Saturday mornings. He had her lie face down, naked on the carpet under the new hoist, and began to buckle a series of black leather belts around her body: over and under her breasts, around her waist, just below her ass, at her knees, and at her ankles. He bent her knees, forcing her ankles toward her ass. He attached the hoist cable to her ankles, then to the rest of the belts.

He tied Kim's wrists and elbows behind her back with soft cotton rope, fixing her in a hog-tie position. Finally, he touched the up button on the winch and lifted this beautiful woman package to about four feet from the floor.

"Open that ravishing mouth of yours, my dear." He touched her chin and held up the rubber ball gag in his other hand. Kim grinned and swallowed hard to accept the gag. The gag eased into her mouth behind her teeth as usual, and Bryan buckled the leather strap behind her head.

He could see the lust in her face, her pleading eyes as he let go of her chin. Her head lowered, causing her soft mane to cover her face. Her body's weight was now her bondage. He gave her a gentle push and watched her swing and turn slowly, uncontrollably.

"I almost forgot," he said. He opened a small box, pulled out a small, but impressive vibrator, and turned it on high. The familiar buzz echoed in the quiet, peaceful room. Kim knew what he was going to do; she only hoped her pussy was lubricated enough to handle his little play toy.

"This should keep you busy for a while," he said approvingly.

He took his time playing with her slit, easing the hard vibrating rubber rod just inside and then out again several times. Her excitement rose as he teased her slit, and she wondered when he was going to put that delicious thing deep inside her. By now, her pussy was dripping wet and ready; he opened her lips with his left hand and inserted the incredible rod as far into her depths as it would go.

The muscles of her vagina reluctantly accepted the insertion. "Ugh!" she grunted from behind the gag. Soon though, her muscles relaxed and the immediate pain turned into immense pleasure.

The vibrator's soft buzz sent waves of delight throughout her body and provided a constant source of pleasure. This was what she lived for: to be totally helpless, forced to endure a sexual intrusion and unable to stop it.

"Oh yes," Bryan said. "I think this piece of duct tape will work just fine." He taped the vibrator into her pussy, running the tape from just below her belly button down to the beginning crack of her ass. "We don't want our little buddy to come out, now, do we?" he asked.

Seemingly satisfied with his handiwork. Bryan touched the up button on the hoist control to lift her a few feet higher. Her body swung slightly at the end of the long cable. Such a beautiful sight to see that lovely body swing in suspension.

"There, my dear. You look comfortable, but I have one other thing for you. As you know, I just love nipple clamps." Her face turned pale, in pure desperation, her eyes pleading for a little mercy. "Yes, these will do just fine." he selected a pair of Japanese clamps. "A little adjustment, and there we go." He clipped one onto her rigid right nipple.

"Ahee!" A muffled scream escaped from behind the gag. He completed his task with another clamp to her left nipple. "Ahee!" Another squeal erupted from behind the gag.

"My beautiful Kim, the look in those glistening eyes of yours is priceless. I know you're a treasure. Now for the weights." She tried to struggle, but her body just swayed back and forth on the cable. "Six ounces on each nipple will work; I'm quite sure you can handle this."

Bryan used s-hooks to attach a weight to each nipple clamp, and they began to swing with her body. "I know you adore a challenge, and I think you'll remember this one for a long time. Let's see," he said, looking at his watch. "It's about nine and my meeting is at ten. I should be home around twelve. Enjoy!"

Bill Majors and Greg Jeffers were seated in the plush leather chairs in Bill's office, waiting for Bryan. "Ah, yes, good morning, Bryan," Bill said as he entered the office. "Have a seat." They shook hands, a little cigar smoke floating in the room from Greg's Panatela.

"Greg was just filling me in on what's going on," Bill said to Bryan.

Bryan sat down in the last leather chair across from the other two men. "Something's up, I can tell. What's going on?" he asked, coming right to the point.

Greg gave him a serious look. "Bryan," he said, "I was very impressed with how you handled yourself at the shipyard that night. Kelly and Peggy said the same thing. Kelly was especially impressed, considering that you saved her life. You saved a lot of lives that night."

"Thank you, sir, for those kind words," Bryan replied, "but I know you didn't call me in here just to tell me that."

"That's what I like about you. Get right to the point. Okay, here it is the old-fashioned way. As you remember, the Company sent Kelly and Peggy to Greece to try and track down the remaining kidnapped women.

"They raided that private island you talked about, a staging point for them, if you will. Everyone had gone except for a few caretakers. During the raid, they found several boxes of documents explaining where the remaining kidnapped women might be and where we might find Rema.

"Both Kelly and Peggy are now in London at our embassy and they've asked for your help researching those documents."

"What sort of documents are we talking about, and why me?" Bryan asked.

"It seems a guy named 'Lord Baltic' may be holding one or more of these women," Greg replied. "His name has shown up several times. It took a while but we tracked him down to a small countryside town just outside of London.

"Kelly feels they have enough evidence to raid Baltic's place, but he's so well liked by the locals that the Brits, in all their glory, feel they need more proof that he's involved. At this point, they won't authorize any type of raid on his estate. The documents are accounting papers, and Kelly feels that with your knowledge of accounting and this ongoing case, you might be able to help uncover what they need."

"Sir, I'd be honored to help in any way, as long as Bill doesn't mind. I still work for him, you know."

"Don't worry about your job here. We can hold things down," Bill assured him.

"It's settled, then," Greg smiled. "I'll send a car to pick you up around six tonight. There's a private jet for you that will be ready when you get to the airport. Kelly and Peggy will meet you when you arrive. Good luck and good hunting."

Bryan returned home at about noon, as he had told Kim, and immediately checked on her condition. Still positioned just as he'd left her, she seemed to be patiently content where she was. When she heard him enter the room, she tried to shift her head to see him.

Bryan walked to the hoist control and lowered her to the level of his cock. Then he positioned himself behind her, unstrapped her legs and retied each ankle to wall hooks on opposite sides of the room. Her legs now spread wide, offered easy access to her glorious ass and pussy.

Bryan ripped away the tape that held the vibrator in place. "I just love these new batteries. They just keep running," he said approvingly, the vibrator still buzzing away.

Kim gasped in relief when the vibrator came out of her vaginal prison. Her pussy, under such stress for so long, had provided her with one orgasm after another. She was lost in total lust.

Bryan could see that she had been sweating for some time, and he hoped she was ready for her next challenge. He removed his clothes and stepped in front of her. "Let's get that ball gag out." He unbuckled the strap and dislodged the gag from her mouth. She slowly closed her mouth after licking her lips.

She pulled her head up and looked directly at his cock—he was stroking it. She loved watching him masturbate; it made her feel incredibly womanly to see that she excited him so much.

"I guess I know what you're gonna do now," Kim said, her voice a little hoarse after having that rubber ball in her mouth for so long. She continued to watch as his cock's head turned purple and it stood at attention like a stature.

He didn't say anything but grabbed her hair and pulled her head towards his cock. She opened her mouth and her hot tongue touched his cock as he pushed it in. She closed her lips around the shaft and started to work her mouth up and down its length, only stopping to lick the folds of skin around the swollen head.

"Ah!" He gritted his teeth at the amazing sensation. Her hot mouth was so wet and wanting that he knew it wouldn't be long before he came. This time, he wanted something else, so he stopped the blowjob, to her disappointment, and moved between her spread legs.

He continued stroking his cock as he gazed at her wet pussy, his hard cock bobbing up and down with each stroke. He rubbed the head against her clit, teasing it before he entered her sex. Then, as she shivered with the contact, he rammed his man hood deep into her channel.

"Ugh!" She gasped. "Go deeper! Please! I can feel you against the walls of my cunt." He began to pump in and then out; her warmth and wetness around his cock aided his relentless drive to her inner core.

He gritted his teeth and pushed deeper into Kim's helpless hot pussy, then slowly pull his cock out to the edge of the opening and then slammed it deep inside her again. "My God, you're good! I just can't stop." He stopped only long enough to retrieve his small handled whip and started pumping again. This time, as he thrust in, he struck her ass with the whip.

"Ahee!" she squealed, not expecting the hit. A red mark quickly appeared on her skin. Her body tensed, yet the excitement magnified the sexual sensation. He waited for her to relax and then lashed her other ass cheek with the whip; another red mark joined the first.

"Ahee!" she squealed again. "Again! Do it again!" A third stroke made contact where the first one had landed. "*Ahee!*" She threw her head to one side and her body stiffened, her hair flying in all directions at once. He felt her wetness explode against his member, and he knew she had just come all over his cock.

Rema's Revenge

With both hands on her hips, he pulled himself deep into her pussy and held his cock in place as his load erupted deep into her body. Lustfully, he gasped for air.

After their bodies recovered from the massive orgasm, he let her down and removed the restraints. The nipple clamps and weights were the last to come off.

"I didn't think I could handle the clamps any more," she said in a strained voice. "The pull sent streams of fire through my breasts: I've felt it before, but this time, being suspended, it just burned so. It never let up."

"I knew you could handle it." Bryan smiled. "My dear, some women are made for bondage, and you are at the top of the list. I know you love it."

Kim shrugged and nodded in her usual sexy manner, her hair falling to one side.

"What did Mr. Jeffers want?" she asked.

"It seems that Kelly and Peggy have unearthed some documents about the remaining kidnapped women. They raided that island near Greece and found a lot of information about a guy named 'Lord Baltic.' If my memory serves me right, he was at the Level Three auction several months ago—the same one Rema was at with you."

"Man, do I remember Rema," she said. "I don't think I'll ever forget that night. I made a lot of money, but it was a night of nights. By the way, how did you know about that auction?"

"Kelly and I were the observers that night," he said. "They didn't want you to know." Kim shook her head, but said nothing.

Bryan continued, "Kelly said they tracked Baltic down to a little town near London, and that's where they are now. They want me to research those papers, and maybe I can get some more proof that this guy Baltic is truly involved. They're sending a car for me at six—I need to pack."

"How long will you be gone?" Kim's heart skipped a beat. Her eyes glazed a bit to think that he would be leaving.

"Maybe a couple of weeks, no more. I'll be back—I can assure you of that," he promised.

"That's a long time for me to be without some attention, if you know what I mean?" Kim said.

"Would you like me to call Pat Howard for you? She really wants you, you know. Only if you want to—it's up to you."

"I've never been with a woman like that before. It might be a lot of fun. Only if you approve?" she said an innocent little-girl look in her eyes.

"My darling little slut slave, I'll set it up."

The Search (Chapter 2)

She watched as her Master's car disappeared down the gravel road, wondering what adventures lay ahead for her with Pat. It was going to be a long two weeks until he returned, and that was still an if. In any case he had made the appointment for her with Pat, and maybe that would make his absence a little less stressful.

The long flight was uneventful, but Bryan was somewhat surprised when the plane taxied to a stop in front of an isolated private hangar some distance from the main terminal. It only took a few minutes for the ground crew to set some steps to the door so he could leave the plane.

He walked out onto the tarmac and into a very dark night with a light mist in the air. An attendant took his suitcase and briefcase and told him he would get them back in just a few minutes. Standing in front of him were Kelly and Peggy, just as beautiful as ever; they had a limo with the door open.

"Hey, guy!" Kelly called to him. "Don't worry about your bags. It'll only take a minute for customs to clear you; they already know who you are. We'll pick them up in front when we drive around."

"Hey yourself," he responded. "It's great to see you. Nice limo." All he could think about was that lovely body of Kelly's and that night she had spent locked and tortured in one of Rema's shipping containers.

"Hi, Bryan!" Peggy winked at him and flicked her brown hair out of her eyes. Her voice brought back another memory of the night he had spend tied and gagged on her bed and the field day she and Pat Howard had had with his body. Some night that had been.

"My dear Peggy!" He greeted her with a wave. "I talked to an old friend of yours yesterday. She said to say hello."

"And who might that be?" she responded with a smile as lovely as ever.

"Pat Howard. I'm sure you remember her."

Apparently the name had some effect on her; she nodded her head and giggled. "How could I ever forget her? She's a very good woman and a very good friend."

"Enough chatter, guys," Kelly said. "Let's get your luggage, Bryan; it's getting late and we've got an early meeting in the morning with the ambassador."

The trip took them through London's downtown and the Soho district, where Kelly pointed out the many hot spots since it was Bryan's first time in London. "This is Piccadilly, Bryan. We're down the street from the Circus area."

Soon the driver turned the limo onto Regent Street, then into a very large gated complex, and stopped in front of the guard station. Kelly rolled the window down as a big Marine sentry approached and kicked his heels to attention.

"Good evening, Miss Kelly and Miss Peggy," the well-dressed Marine greeted them. He had just started to inspect the car when he saw Bryan. "This must be Mr. Wescott?"

"Ah, yes it is, Jerry," Kelly said, sitting back in her seat so he could get a better look.

"Mr. Wescott, we've been expecting you," the Marine said. "Welcome to the United States in London. I have an ID badge for you. If you leave the grounds, present this and whoever is on duty will let you back in."

Bryan took the badge and the driver pulled away. A minute later he parked at the back of the large fenced estate.

"Follow me, Bryan," Kelly said. "We have a nice suite for you, for as long as you need it. Peggy and I will fetch you around nine for breakfast and then take you to the meeting at ten with the ambassador.

The following morning, the three of them proceeded down the large corridor toward what Bryan knew to be the ambassador's office. They entered through a massive English—style door that reminded Bryan of a medieval castle entrance. On the door, a sign read, "The Ambassador to the United States." Kelly opened the door, and they walked in.

A well-dressed older lady with graying hair was sitting behind a large mahogany desk with papers scattered everywhere. She looked up and greeted them as they entered. "Good morning, Kelly, Peggy, this must be our Mr. Wescott?"

"Good morning, Sara Jean," Kelly responded. "Yes, this is Bryan Wescott. Bryan, this is Sara Jean, the ambassador's personal secretary."

"Nice to meet you, Mr. Wescott," she said, offering her hand and smiling. As always, Bryan returned the handshake and the smile respectfully.

"The ambassador will be with you shortly," Sara Jean told them. "Just have a seat."

A few minutes later they entered the main office, and seated behind another large desk was Ambassador John Springer. "Good morning, all," he said as everyone took a seat. "Mr. Wescott, it's nice to meet you. Greg Jeffers has told me a great deal about you, and I must say, a lot of very interesting things."

"Thank you, sir," Bryan responded. "Mr. Jeffers is a very good man."

"That he is son, yes, that he is," the ambassador replied.

"Bryan, you're here because Kelly and Peggy have unearthed some disturbing evidence linking a Brit named Lord Baltic to this Tony Rema fellow. We have reason to believe he's holding one or two of the women Rema kidnapped almost a year ago. The local officials here don't think we have enough evidence to go raiding his estate. They have said they need more, and that's where you come in."

"Sir!" the speakerphone sounded, "Mr. Bromley is here. Shall I send him in?"

Mr. Bromley entered the office and the Ambassador made the introductions. Bryan could tell that he was some sort of legal counsel from his polished suit and the way he presented himself.

"Mr. Bromley is our British legal envoy," the ambassador said. "He has been assigned to help us in our evidence-gathering and to make sure we follow their policies. Mr. Bromley, please tell us what we need to get an order to go get this guy."

"Well sir," Bromley said in a polished British accent, "you see, we must be able to directly tie Baltic to Rema and to the women in question. The paperwork that Kelly and Peggy found may give us the leads we need to do this. We cannot proceed until I can get approval from a judge for a raid."

"Sir," Bryan interrupted, "what makes this guy Baltic so important that we have to have so much proof?"

"Good question, Mr. Wescott," Bromley responded. "You see sir, the local people in his town like him a lot. He has put a lot of money into their schools, hospitals, and things like that. If we just go in there without enough proof we could upset several high members of parliament. We don't want to do that."

"I guess, then, I need to get to work on those boxes of files Kelly and Peggy found," Bryan suggested.

"Very good, Bryan," the ambassador said. "Kelly and Peggy will get you started. We have a room downstairs already set up for you."

"Thank you sir," Bryan replied. "Mr. Bromley, if I come up with something, I'll let you know. Okay, Kelly, let's get to work."

The room was located in the basement of the complex. Bryan looked around as he entered. The gray cinder block walls reminded him of a jail cell; the only difference was that the room was set up with tables, chairs, and a computer. He was glad to see a vent and noticed that the air conditioner was working.

Five file boxes were sitting on the table, waiting for his attention. "If you find something, just let me know," Kelly said. "There's a phone on the far table; just punch 21 and I'll pick up."

Bryan spent the rest of the day searching the mountain of files, memos, invoices, and receipts that filled the boxes. When he found a page of interest, he would set it aside. If another page came up with similar information, he would add it to the pile.

The second day was more of the same: more copies of files and documents depicting Rema's movements and his sales of weapons and women to the Arabs. He remembered that eighteen women had been kidnapped, but only eight had been rescued after his adventure of the ship, not including Kelly and Christy. That left ten women unaccounted for.

On the third morning, Bryan finally pieced together some information that Bromley needed to know. He called Kelly.

"What's up, Bryan? Find something?" she asked, excited that he might be on to something.

"You need to get Bromley and get down here. I think I may have something for you," he reported.

"We're on our way. Bromley just left the ambassador's office. See you in five." The phone went dead.

"Okay, what you got, Bryan," Kelly asked, when they arrived. Bromley and Peggy sat down at the table.

"Please do not move any of those papers in front of you; I have them in a specific order," Bryan informed everyone. Then he opened his notebook. "It seems that a man named Lee Suko was in charge of Rema's island, the one you raided. Rema didn't own the island—he leased it on a yearly agreement from a real estate company here in London. He paid one million American dollars a year for the lease.

This guy Suko is a colonel in the North Korean army and is in partnership with Rema. These documents support that and the sale of illegal weapons to the North Koreans as well. Most of the arms sales and the sale of the women were directed by Suko. Lord Baltic is also in partnership with Rema and works as a go-between for Rema and a guy in Northern England, some guy named Ivan Ross. Does that name ring any bells?"

"My God yes!" Bromley jumped to his feet. "Do you know where he is? Ross is one of the most wanted men in the country? I can't tell you how many people he's killed or had killed."

"No, unfortunately, I don't know where he is," Bryan said, "but from these documents, he has visited Baltic at his estate and I suspect he may have at least two of those kidnapped women. There are invoices that indicate Ross has bought arms and ammo from Rema and Baltic delivered them.

"Baltic is a very clever person and has done some very interesting things to cover up his activities. As you said, the locals admire him, and he knows that. He uses that to draw attention away from the operation, and he doesn't want to upset that.

"There's more," Bryan continued, shuffling papers on the desk. "There is a furniture company somewhere in London called 'Lourans Furniture Limited.' Do either of you know the place?"

"Yes," Bromley spoke up. "I know the place, and they make some very fine and expensive furniture. They're widely known in Britain."

"That they do," Bryan agreed. "It also seems they have a back room where they make some very plush bondage and torture furniture. They've shipped a lot of it to Suko on Rema's island. At least five pieces of this furniture were sent back to Baltic on one of Rema's ships."

"Why didn't Baltic just go into London and buy the furniture himself instead of doing all that shipping?" Bromley seemed confused. "Also, how can you track these shipments?"

"Anonymity," Bryan continued. "Baltic would never be questioned about making a purchase from Greece, but buying something like this in London would be a lot easier to trace by someone local. It just stands out.

Tracking the shipments? That was easy. This company is exclusive—a coded brass number label is located somewhere on each piece of furniture. It's a one-of-a-kind thing. They do it with all their furniture."

"How do you know that?" Bromley asked, wiping sweat off his face.

"I called a friend of mine in the U.S. named Nick Baxter. He's purchased some special pieces from them, and he gave me the inside scoop. The invoices reflect five special pieces of furniture, all labeled with ship dates and destination points that were sent to Baltic. The documents reflect that he made a trip to a construction firm in South Florida about two months before two women were kidnapped. These women both worked for the same construction firm. It all corresponds. I think he now owns these two women, and he's using that furniture on them," Bryan said.

"He also has five rounded metal cages big enough for a person to stand up in. At least five women were shipped to him from the island in those cages and sealed in wood crates. The metal cages were done the same way as the furniture: a company named 'Harm's Metal Works Limited' did the construction and then shipped them to Suko.

"Baltic may not have all of the women now. Ross visited him a few months after he received the large shipment from Suko. Two of the crates were labeled 'IR'—they were earmarked for Ivan Ross. I suspect that he picked up his guns and his two women. Of course, we really won't know that until we can get inside Baltic's house. We'll need to find that furniture."

"If I go to the judge administrator, he'll ask me how I know the furniture Baltic received was actually bondage furniture instead of, say, something like a desk? The cages could just be decorations in his house."

"Good question, Bromley," Bryan replied. "We need to confront the owners of both companies and research their files for the type of furniture and the label numbers. That will tell us the exact types of furniture, and cages, and I can reference whether this furniture was in those crates. Can we get a court order to look at their records?"

"Absolutely!" Bromley replied. "Kelly, get the car, and I'll be with you in ten minutes."

Thirty minutes later Kelly, Peggy, Bryan, and Bromley were standing in the middle of Lourans Furniture waiting on the owner. Bromley quickly showed him their request, and with much disdain, he showed them into the back room and went to get the files.

Bryan was impressed with the layout of the room and the expertise of the two men working on more of the fabulous bondage furniture. He thought about using some of it in his basement and how nice Kim would look tied to some of it.

The owner returned with the files he had requested, and handed the documents to Bryan. After a few minutes he was able to match his numbers to the company's information. "Ah, yes, here we are." Bryan hesitated for a few seconds. "As I suspected: a stretching rack with all the restraints; two different styles of spanking benches; one with head and wrists stocks. This is a unique piece because it also has ankle stocks. The fourth piece of equipment is an 'X' frame with special attachments for suspension, head up or down. The fifth piece is some sort of special chair."

"Can you tell me about the chair?" Bryan asked the company owner.

The owner introduced Bryan to the man who had made the chair, and he described the chairs special controls and functions. It could be used as a bondage chair or a control chair for other functions. Bryan was impressed with the lecture and the construction techniques.

With their suspensions realized, they were off to the metal works for another round of comparing invoices to find the cages. Again, Bryan was impressed with the cages' solid construction; they could keep anyone prisoner.

"Okay, Bromley," Bryan said. "Do we have enough information for your judge?"

"I certainly think so, especially with the information about Ivan Ross. Let's go see the judge administrator." Bromley seemed excited. "Kelly, you and Peggy let the ambassador know of our find."

Bromley's meeting with the judge administrator lasted about fifteen minutes. Then the judge told Bromley he would have to wait in the lobby with Bryan until he finally made his decision.

"How'd it go, Bromley?" Bryan asked.

"I'm not sure, sir," he replied, "I'm rather confused. He told me to wait while he reviewed the information."

An hour later, a security guard told Bromley and Bryan to step into the judge's chambers. "Mr. Bromley and Mr. Wescott," the judge greeted the men. "I have reviewed your request for a raid on Lord Baltic's residence. As you are aware, some of the members of Parliament are very concerned about this because of Baltic's contributions to the local townsfolk. However, with the proof of Ivan Ross being personally involved, I have no choice but to grant you your request."

"Thank you, sir." Bromley took the documents. "Let's go and get this thing started, Bryan."

The Raid (Chapter 3)

Kelly and Peggy had the full backing of the ambassador as they left the embassy and headed for a rendezvous with the strike team. The sound was deafening as the four large Huey military helicopter gunships filled with Rangers picked up Kelly, Peggy, Bryan, and Bromley. In a flash the engines picked up speed, they lifted off from the nearby base, and they were on their way to the country estate of Lord Baltic.

Three helicopters landed in a field next to the house and immediately the Ranges with weapons at the ready moved across the yard towards the main house. Others scattered toward the outbuildings surrounding the house. The fourth helicopter, containing Kelly and the group, continued to fly around the others as they waited for the rangers to take control of the large estate house.

The radio call came in that the house was secure and they were in control. The captain reported no fire, and only a few staff were present in the main house. They reported that Lord Baltic was nowhere to be found. The fourth helicopter landed, and they entered the old majestic house.

Several minutes went by with no one able to find any indication that anything was out of the ordinary. "Let's talk to the staff," Bryan declared with a scowl on his face. "I want to know where this guy Baltic went."

Bryan sat down behind an expensive-looking mahogany desk and told the Captain to bring the staff members in one at a time to sit in front of him.

Several Rangers stood beside Bryan, with Kelly and Bromley close by; Peggy had left the three to investigate upstairs. Bryan hoped the display would be intimidating enough to force someone to speak up.

"Where's Baltic?" Bryan's voice was undeviating. The young housemaid who was first to enter was almost in tears with fear.

"Sir," she said, "two hours before you got here, Lord Baltic received a phone call and almost ran out of the house. His plane was full of petrol, so he was able to take off almost immediately. Sir, I do not know where he was going, nor do any of the others."

"I'll be damned!" Bryan blurted out in disgust, turning to Bromley. "I'll bet you that damn judge called Baltic. That was why it took so long for him to give us an answer. It gave him an opportunity to escape this raid. If he left in that big of a hurry, I know there's something wrong here. We need to look closer."

"Excuse me, Captain," a Ranger said, appearing at the room's entrance. "Sir, we've been through the house and outbuildings and have found nothing. We did find a landing strip where a small plane was kept."

"Thank you, Corporal," the Captain said. "Just continue to look around and *don't* leave anything unturned."

Bryan sat back in the high-back leather chair and looked around the room. Large stately paintings and gothic sculptures were everywhere. A small fire in the fireplace made the room feel cozy and seemed to fit the kind of house that an aristocrat would live in. This man had money, and a lot of it; Bryan knew he could afford anything he wanted.

"Kelly," Bryan asked, "didn't Baltic attend the level three auction several months ago?"

"Yes, he sure did," Kelly replied. "From what Pat told me, he was almost as sadistic as Rema was with Kim."

"A man like that has a lot to hide, especially after all the information we got from those documents." Bryan could feel there was much more. He started examining the desk, pulling each drawer out and looking under the desktop. To his amazement, he saw a number etched on a brass label.

"Captain, can you get a call into London?" Bryan asked. "I need to talk to the owner of Lourans Furniture Limited as soon as possible."

"Absolutely. It will only take a few minutes." The captain gestured to his radio operator.

"What are you thinking, Bryan?" Kelly asked.

"Kelly, this desk was made by Lourans, and I think there are some controls built into it. If I talk to the guy who made this desk, it might help us."

"Lourans owner is on the line, sir." The captain handed the phone to Bryan.

"Sir, this is Bryan Wescott. We spoke earlier this morning. Do you remember me?"

"Yes, Mr. Wescott, I do remember you and the group of people who accosted my business this morning. How could I forget?"

"Sir, I'm sitting at a very large mahogany desk in Lord Baltic's study. There is a number on a brass label under the top, and I need all the information you have on this piece of furniture."

"I thought you were only interested in bondage furniture," the owner replied.

"Not this piece. This is a little different." Bryan said.

"What's the number?"

Bryan gave him the five-digit number, and several minutes passed before the owner returned to the phone. "Mr. Wescott, are you still there?" the man asked.

"Yep! Still here," Bryan said. "What you got for me?"

"I talked to Mike. Look at the right drawer and try to pull it open. It's a false drawer and you won't be able to open it. Turn the handle counterclockwise one half-turn, and a small panel will open just above the drawer and below the top of the desk. There should be three buttons."

Bryan followed his instructions and the control panel appeared. "Can you tell me what these buttons do before I start pushing them?"

"I'm not sure. They're made to fit several different applications—maybe to open a door or turn on a light or something like that. We just build it; the customer has it modified to fit his own needs."

"Thanks. Just wish me luck." Bryan hung the phone up. "Okay, Kelly, let's just see what these things do. Captain, you got your people ready?"

With everyone in place, Bryan pushed button number one. Immediately the fire in the gas fireplace went out. "Let's try number two." This time, to the amazement of the entire group, the entire fireplace swung open to expose a hidden passage. "How about that?" Bryan exclaimed.

The third button turned a light on inside the passage. "Let's check it out," he said, walking over to the opening in the wall. The others followed. Immediately they encountered a stone staircase that led them down into a large hallway. Bryan flipped on another light on the wall just inside the door that illuminated the entire hall.

On his left was a stone wall that went to the ceiling, but on his right he saw a large wooden door, tightly padlocked. "Captain, we need to break that lock," Bryan said. Within seconds, the lock was broken and Bryan opened the heavy walnut door to reveal a totally dark room. He found another switch just inside the door; the dim light illuminated a dungeon.

The room was empty of people but a spanking bench sat idle in the middle of the room. A damp leather smell filled the stone room, emanating from a rack on the wall filled with whips of every description. There were several pairs of leather cuffs hanging next to the whips, and various lengths of rope hung next to the leather cuffs.

Bryan inspected the spanking bench and found the brass label with the number that corresponded to the invoice numbers he was looking for. In the corner was a large birdcage that matched the style he had viewed from the Metal Company. He was very impressed with its construction and ability to keep a prisoner a prisoner.

"Sir," one of the rangers spoke up, "there are more rooms down the hall and they are all locked."

"I wonder what's behind door number two?" Bryan asked as they all moved to the next room.

They broke another lock and found another dim light that exposed a similar room: Stone walls, damp, dark, smelling strongly of leather, but with an "X" frame in the middle of the room bolted to the floor. There were more whips and chains, but this time a slight movement caught his attention from the cage in the corner. A woman was locked in it.

He could see her eyes blinking several times in the transition from total darkness to sudden light. Her long black silky hair gleamed in the dim light as it lay across her shoulder. Her dark slanted eyes grew wide with fear at the sight of Bryan as he moved closer to the cage. The others stood at the door and watched.

She was naked, and her wrists were cuffed, elevated just above her head, and bolted together to the iron bars of the cage. Her ankles were locked in the same fashion, which forced her to spread her legs, offering an interesting view of her hairless slit. The ball gag tightly buckled behind her head gave her no chance to speak or ask what was going to happen to her next.

Bryan surveyed her sleek olive-skinned body, shivering both from the dampness in the room and her impossible helpless condition. Her small breasts and hard nipples jutted forward and then back with her labored breathing.

It was plain to see that she was Asian and did not fit the description of any of the women that were missing. He watched her for a few seconds, wondering what Kim would do if she were in this position. It was an interesting thought.

"We need to get her out of there, buddy." Kelly touched Bryan's shoulder.

"She is lovely, isn't she?" he remarked. "Yes, yes it's okay he said in a soft voice," looking into her lost face. "We're here to help. Captain, let's get her out of that cage."

One of the troops retrieved a camouflage suit from one of the helicopters and Kelly helped her get dressed. "Do you speak English?" Bryan asked her.

"Yes, me speak English." Her voice was weak from the ache in her jaws from the gag.

"What's your name?"

"Me Torry Nishi. Me from Japan," she said. "Mr. Chi Ling is my Grandfather, he own auto parts company in Japan, and he pay you for rescue me."

"I'll be damned! Kelly, this is Chi's granddaughter," Bryan said, stunned at the information. "Yes, my dear, I know him. He's one of my clients. Kelly, we need to let Bill know so he can call Chi and let him know we found her." Bryan looked back at Torry. "Torry, how did you get here and how long have you been here?" he asked.

"Don't tell Grandfather, please. Me work for Mama Sandju at her Pleasure House in Japan. Me like get tied up; customers pay big money to tie up Torry and play with her. Many girls work at Mama Sandju's house and get tied up, make lots money. One night man from Korea, his name Colonel Suko, ties me up. Another man came in room, he say his name Baltic and want to play with Torry. When Torry left to go home, men grab me and take me to a ship. I heard men say Rema make big money deal for Torry. Much later they take me and lock me in cage. They seal me in a big crate and bring me here. I've been here long time," she finished her story.

"Okay," Bryan said. "Go with one of these troops; he'll see you get on one of the helicopters." He checked the number on the "X" frame, and again it corresponded with his invoice numbers. "Captain, let's check the rest of these rooms."

They unlocked the third door and entered another dungeon room. The room was empty, but another spanking bench was in the middle of the room; this one had the stocks attached to it. It matched the number on the list.

The room was laid out in the same fashion as the other two, with a birdcage in the corner sitting beside another large selection of whips and chains hanging on the wall. Bryan noticed that this cage was a little different than the ones he had seen at the Metal Company: it was bolted to the floor and had metal cuffs welded to the bars for ankles and wrists. Baltic must have added those after he got them to his house, or maybe the builders hadn't shown him all the details, Bryan thought.

The fourth room was also empty of people, and as in the other rooms, another cage sat in the corner bolted to the floor. In the middle of the room was a tie beam with chains attached on each side at the top of the beam. The beam was about four feet tall with its base bolted to a platform on the floor. A black leather neck collar hung to one side of the beam. He could see where the woman would stand, and with the collar around her neck, her body would be bent to offer a very good view of her ass and pussy. It would be a nice target for a whip. This label did not match with the fourth piece of furniture; there were still two more left.

A trooper entered the room and told the captain there was no more rooms, but the hall seemed to extend much further than the room they were in. Then Bryan noticed a door at the far end of the room. He tried the handle, and to his surprise, it opened.

The dim light illuminated a fifth dungeon room, much like the others, with another piece of bondage furniture in the middle of the room. This was the stretching rack he was looking for, with all the chains attached to a ship's wheel. When the wheel turned, the chains would tighten, and the poor woman on the rack would have her arms and legs pulled as tight as you wanted.

The most important thing about this room was another naked woman secured in the birdcage. She was held in place just as Torry had been, with metal cuffs bolted around her wrists and ankles and welded to the bars.

This time, however, a metal collar encircled her neck with rings welded on all four sides. A chain went from each ring to the bars of the cage. She could barely move her head, and there was a ball gag in her mouth. Bryan noticed how tightly the leather straps cut into her cheeks: she was powerless to speak.

She was definitely American, and with a fabulous body. He was almost envious of Baltic, with such a beauty as his house sex slave. This woman was not quite as good-looking as his Kim, but it was plain to see she was a piece of artwork.

It took several minutes to free her from the cuffs and chains.

"What's your name, dear?" Kelly asked her when she was free.

"My name's Tammy Goode: Penny Chandler and I work for Mitchell's Construction Company in Florida. We've been here for a very long time."

"Yes, we know," Kelly said. "We've been looking for you two for almost a year now."

"That bastard Baltic visited our firm and two months later, a guy named Ray Darling and some of his men kidnapped me," Tammy told them. "They got me going to my car one night after work; Penny the same way."

"Ray Darling?" Kelly asked suspicious of the information she had just heard. "You don't know if he had a brother, do you?"

"You know," Tammy said, trying to recall as she put on a camouflage suit, "now that you mention it, I do believe I heard someone say he had a brother named Ted and someone had killed his brother on a ship one night. I was happy to hear about that."

"Small world, ain't it, Kelly?" Bryan said listening to her story. "Tammy, how did you get here?"

"Same as all the others. You see, there were five of us. We were all put in cages like this one and crated up. That bastard Baltic paid a guy named Rema a lot of money for Penny and me."

"How do you know it was Ray Darling that took you?" he asked.

"When Baltic visited our firm, Rema and Ray were with him. We did a write-up on a job for them, and Rema paid for it. It was a dredging operation and a very large roof cover over a waterway that led to the ocean. The cover was big enough for a small ship. I recognized Ray the night I was kidnapped."

"Please continue," Bryan said.

"Somewhere near the Everglades, Rema has a big house close to the ocean. We never sent our people to do the work; he contracted someone else to do it. That was where he took me and Penny and put us on a submarine.

"We wound up on some island near Greece and spent I don't know how many days in the hold of that ship. That's where we were put in these cages, sealed up, and shipped here. We've been kept as sex slaves for the almighty Baltic and his assistant Ulga. They have made us do some very nasty things. He would take one of us whenever he felt the need, and I can't tell you how many times I've been whipped and raped."

"Who's this Ulga?" Kelly seemed surprised.

"She's the one that took care of feeding us and seeing that we got clean and used the bathroom. Then she would assist Baltic in his little games. The worst one for me was when they would tie my wrists to the beam overhead and almost suspend me. Then they would spread my legs and secure my ankles to this bar, and my pussy would be wide open. Baltic would use a whip on my back and ass while Ulga would put this vibrator in my pussy. The damn thing had a button that she would press, and the part that was in me had two little electric tips.

"They would take turns: Baltic would strike me with his whip and I would jerk, then Ulga would push the button and the electric shock inside me made me jerk. They would keep this up until Baltic got tired of using the whip; then they would trade places and start all over again." Tammy paused. "Have you found all the women?" she asked. "You see, there were five of us who were brought here."

"So far, only two: you and an Asian girl named Torry," Kelly said. "You said there were five of you?"

"Yes, that's right. Torry was the Asian. Then there were Linda Grey, Shelly Strong, and Penny Chandler; she's still here, upstairs. I think a guy named Ivan Ross took Linda and Shelly."

"Upstairs?" Bryan asked. "We've had people all over upstairs and haven't found anything."

"Why don't you try the elevator? Just open that door." She gestured to a wooden door at the far end of the room. "Baltic's got two big rooms off from his bedroom. That's where he takes us some of the time when he wants a blowjob or to rape one of us. From that cage, I could see him take each woman upstairs."

Bryan opened the door to the small elevator and found it only big enough for two people. "Tammy, go with the Ranger—he'll get you to the helicopter. Kelly, you and Bromley go up to Baltic's bedroom. The captain and I will go up this thing and find out where it goes."

The captain touched the up button to the elevator, and as soon as it stopped, he opened the door to look directly at Penny Chandler, naked and suspended by her wrists from a wide spreader bar hanging from the ceiling. Her arms and legs were stretched by two more bars. The bar that held her ankles and legs apart had a small hook in the middle with a chain attached to it, fastened to another hook in the floor. She was stretched about as tight as she could get. A ball gag was in her mouth and buckled behind her head, which kept her from making much sound.

Bryan could see numerous whip marks on her beautiful body, especially the red lines that marked her strong and firm breasts and tight nipples. Her pussy and upper thighs sported red flat welts that Bryan recognized as coming from a crop. "He must have had a field day with her," he thought.

As he and the captain let her down, he noticed the wounds on her ass and back. It looked as though Baltic had taken a knife and carved his initials into her skin. The marks would heal in time.

Bryan found the button that opened the hidden door to Baltic's bedroom and was immediately joined by the others.

"Bryan," Peggy asked, "do you remember the big chair at the furniture store?"

"How could I forget that chair?" he replied.

"Well, Baltic has that same chair in the middle of his bedroom, facing the hidden door. He can see right into the room. I wonder how many times he just sat there and watched one of these women hanging from that cable?"

"If I ever get a chance, I'll ask him," Bryan said. He moved over to Penny. "Penny, we have Torry and Tammy—they're all okay. You were the last one to see Baltic—can you tell us about his leaving? We're getting some medical help for you; just take it easy."

"I'm sorry. What's going on? I'll try to help," she said. Baltic's whipping had taken a toll on her, and she was really hurting. "About that chair, you're right. Sometimes Baltic would sit in it for the longest time while Ulga would use her special toy on my pussy. She'd shove that vibrator of hers in me as far as she could get it and press a little button on the outside end. The shock was really bad: I'd jerk and scream and all Baltic would do is laugh and jack off all over himself.

"Baltic was whipping my back and Ulga was whipping my breasts when one of the staff buzzed his beeper. He opened the main door, but did not shut it. He answered the phone, and I heard him say he appreciated getting the call. It sounded like some important person had called him."

"He immediately called his staff people and told them to get the plane ready because he was going to Greece. After the call, he picked up a few things from his dresser and some papers and came back in and whispered something to Ulga. I pretended that I didn't hear anything. He told me that if I said anything, he'd have me killed.

"He hit me one last time with that damned whip, as hard as he has ever hit me, and I passed out. When I came to, he and Ulga were both gone, and I've been hanging like this ever since."

"Do you know where the other secret room is up here?" Bryan asked, "Tammy said there were two."

"Yes, I do," she responded, her voice gaining some strength as it sank in that she'd been rescued. "See that candle light fixture on the wall? Turn it to the right. I saw him do it once."

Bryan followed her instructions and turned the small fixture. A sliding door opened next to the whip wall rack, and he walked into the other room. "Captain!" he called. "You'd better get in here. I think you need to see this."

The captain followed him. "Bloody hell!" Would you look at all these weapons? There's enough ammo here to start a small war. I've got to get the bomb squad in here right away. Rocket launchers with missiles? I bet most of this stuff was set up for Ivan Ross."

"Okay, guys," Bryan said, smiling. "I think we got what we came after and a little bit more. I think a beer or two is in order!"

Madam Wong's Estate (Chapter 4)

Kelly and Peggy were very pleased with the results of the past four days—the stress had taken its toll on all three of them. Although the ride only lasted thirty minutes, Bryan was relaxing and catching up on old times with Kelly and Peggy as they made their way through the plush and peaceful countryside.

The driver turned the limo off the main road and continued through a large open iron gate, and into a large grove of pine trees. They could smell the sweet pine as they drove down the rocky gravel road. A small building appeared in the distance on the edge of the road.

A guard appeared from the small building. "Ah, yes," he said. "Miss Kelly and Miss Peggy, glad to see you. This must be Mr. Wescott?"

"That's right, Carl. Nice to see you again. Is Madam Wong ready for us?"

"Yes, she gave word to let you pass. Edward is at the front door," he informed her.

At the door, a tall well dressed man greeted them. "Welcome, Miss Kelly and Miss Peggy," he said in a polished British accent. "Please do enter." He opened the big double door. "Madam Wong is in the study. I presume this is Mr. Wescott?" His eyebrows rose a bit as he inspected Bryan, who was standing between the two women.

"That's right, Edward. This is Bryan Wescott; he's our co-worker from America," Kelly informed him.

"Pleasure to meet you, sir. Please," he gestured towards the study, "Madam is waiting."

Bryan followed the group into the lavish room; he was amazed at how much it resembled Baltic's living room. The room was lavishly furnished and decorated with majestic paintings and sculptures. Bryan wondered if he would be able to find a speck of dust anywhere.

An elegant Asian-looking woman was sitting on a stylish loveseat. She was dressed in a polished gray silk business suit, and holding a drink. Her hair was tied in a bun with a fashionable hair tie. Bryan could tell this lady knew her business, whatever it was.

"Edward, I'll ring for you in a few minutes with our package," she said.

"Yes, Mum," he said, "as you wish." he nodded just a bit and left the room.

"My dear ladies," the Asian lady said, "it's lovely to see you again. How is the ambassador these days?"

"He sends his regards, madam," Kelly responded.

"Ah! This must be Mr. Wescott?" Madam asked, offering her hand to Bryan for a handshake.

Bryan was now completely confused. None of this made any sense. Today was supposed to have been a joyride in the country, and now he was sitting in a mansion talking to an Asian friend of the ambassador's. This was not really what he had had in mind. But he shook her hand anyway. "The pleasure is mine." he said.

Madam smiled at Bryan, and touched a small button on the coffee table. Almost immediately, Edward returned to the study, this time with another Asian lady.

She was young, very beautiful, and totally naked. She was also on her hands and knees with Edward leading her by a leash. The leash was attached to a large black leather collar buckled around her tender neck. A ball gag in her mouth was buckled behind her head.

"Mr. Wescott, this is Alex," Madam Wong said. Edward pulled lightly on the leash, stopping her parade. "She's very beautiful, isn't she? She's yours for the rest of the day, or at least until four. Kelly and Peggy thought this was the least they could do for you. They've paid the bill.

"You can do just about anything you want to her," Madam Wong continued, "but just remember, she has other clients later this evening and must be able to serve them. Edward will see to it that you get settled in a room downstairs, and we'll see you again at four."

Edward handed the leash to Bryan. "Thank you," Bryan said. "She's very lovely."

"That she is, sir," Edward commented. "Would you follow me?"

"Ladies, I'll see you later," Bryan said, following Edward and leading the lovely girl by her leash. Kelly and Peggy both smiled.

A few minutes later, they entered a large stone room in the mansion's basement. "No one will bother you here, sir," Edward told Bryan. "All of the equipment is in proper order for your use. If you desire, there are a cart and harness outside the door; Alex can give you a cart ride around the estate. She is very practiced at pulling a cart. I can arrange that for you: just ring the bell on the wall and I'll be in within a few minutes."

"Thank you, Edward. I just might do that." In all his BDSM days, Bryan had never used a pony girl. The prospect was very interesting. First, though, there were other things on his mind.

Alex's long black hair raced down her back like spun silk, glistening in the dim light. He ran his hands through it several times to feel its texture. Her head was still facing down. She was a beauty, though, her skin soft to the touch but still tight. Her athletic body shivered at his light touch.

Her breasts were firm, a little small, but still large enough to make any woman proud. He cupped her right breast and squeezed it. She gasped from the pressure but said nothing. He was fascinated by how well she could take a little pain.

Her rigid nipples jutted forward and slightly up, making her appear more naked than she already was. Bryan stood over her like a warlord ready to devour his captive slave. He knew this was his calling in life: to be a controlled sadist, a man possessed, savagely taking a woman to and beyond her limits, but in reality not causing her bodily damage.

He tugged on her hair, and she lifted her head to face him; he removed the ball gag that was still in her mouth. "Alex, up on your knees," he ordered. She shifted her position and immediately obeyed his command. She watched him closely as he removed his clothes and threw them to the far side of the room.

His cock was already rock hard—he began to stroke it a few times and then put it to her face. "Open your mouth and take it inside." She blinked a couple of times, swallowed once, and followed his order. "Splendid," he said. "I don't want to feel any teeth, do you understand?" She gave a small nod to indicate that she understood.

Her lips touched his cock lightly as he slid it toward the back of her throat. He held the back of her head in his left hand and guided her hot, soft mouth up and down along the shaft. She closed her eyes as he continued his sensuous mouth fuck.

Soon he felt the familiar urge of cum building in his loins, but this was happening way too fast. The day was still young, and the promise of a cart ride still loomed in the back of his mind.

"Okay, Alex, that's enough for now," he said. It was hard to resist coming in her mouth and making her swallow. He was almost sorry he'd said it. She eased the pressure around his shaft, and he backed away from her.

"On the spanking bench, now," he ordered. "Spread that incredible body of yours. I want to lay a little whip on that ass. This could take a while, so put your wrists to the legs in front of the bench and your ankles to the back."

After arranging the leather restraints, he secured her to the bench, prominently displaying her ass and her pussy opened for the whipping. Bryan noticed how lubricated she was around her slit. What a treasure of a woman. Madam Wong had a gold mine in this young and willing slave.

He selected a flogger from the whip rack and tested the condition of the leather for the proper force to be applied. The first stroke was strong, but not as powerful as was to come later. She winced at the strike, but made no sound.

The second stroke was much harder and the third even more so; the sound of leather tines hitting flesh echoed in the room. "*Ahee!*" she squealed. He had reached a level that obtained a response from her. Bryan liked that.

He continued whipping his slave for a long time, leaving no part of her backside unmarked. Finally, though, he wanted to fuck her more than continue to whip her.

He laid the whip down next to the bench and positioned himself just behind her ass, but did not penetrate her sex. Instead, he lay down on the top of her and put his arms around her. He cupped both of her amazing breasts, squeezed them, and torturously pinched her nipples.

"Ahee!" she squealed again at the intense pain and trauma that tormented her body. She tried to adjust her body to Bryan's massive weight, but as she did so, his cock slid into her lovely pussy.

"Oh!" he said, feeling the delicious sensation of her sex that engulfed his cock. "You truly are a treasure, surrendering to my will this way and not being able to stop me in any way. Yes you truly are a treasure."

He continued his assault on her pussy, taking his time to build his orgasm, letting it ease off, then starting again. Time has a way with sex; eventually the body will take control and let loose its incredible display of splendor.

Bryan removed his cock from its feminine prison and moved to her front. With his left hand, he tugged on her black mane and pulled her face up to face his raging member. She opened her waiting mouth and received his cock, lubricated with her own juices.

"When I come, you get it all before you swallow it. You understand me?" he gasped. He still had hold of her hair, but she nodded her head. Seconds later, his cock erupted with a massive dose of cum that shot against the back of her throat.

The tingling sensation gone from his cock, he released her hair and eased his cock out of her mouth. She closed her mouth, but did not swallow his cum. Bryan quickly picked up his whip and struck her ass with a vicious blow.

She gasped for air at the unsuspecting strike and swallowed his cum. He looked at her as she swallowed. "Works every time," he told her.

After a few minutes he released her from her restraints and had her sit down in a small chair. He then poured them both a glass of Scotch. "That should wash down any leftover cum, my dear," he said.

He then pressed the button on the wall for Edward, who entered as requested. "Yes, sir?"

"Edward, I think I'd like that cart ride now. Can we do that?" Bryan asked.

"Yes, sir. I'll get the harness; it's just outside the door. Have Alex put these leather boots on and stand up in the middle of the room for me."

Bryan watched as Edward took an eight-inch leather belt and tightly buckled it around Alex's waist. Attached to the belt at Alex's back were two large leather straps, which he put over her shoulders and crossed between her breasts. He attached the straps to the belt at her front.

Finally he put a leather cuff with a short length of chain attached to it on each of her wrists. "We must remember," Edward informed Bryan, "when we attach these chains to the cart, we need to leave a little play in the chain so she can grab the front handrail."

They stepped outside to the waiting cart, where Edward attached two other chains from the waist belt to the handrails behind her. "Why did you do that, Edward?" Bryan asked.

"You see, sir, she can pull the cart by her hands, her stomach from the front rail, or her back with these chains attached to the rail. She's well secured to the cart.

"Now for the head harness," he said. Bryan watched as Edward put the rubber gag bit into Alex's mouth and buckled it behind her head. Straps came up the side of the bit to attach to another strap over her head. These straps had blinders like he had seen on horses at the racetrack.

"Here're the reins." Edward handed them to Bryan. As he did, he snapped one to each side of the bit. "Sir," Edward continued, "if you want to turn right or left, just pull on the rein to that side. To get her started, just strap her back with both reins and she will walk on. If you want to stop, pull back and she will stop. If she slows down too much, here is a buggy whip; I think you know what to do with that.

"If you stay on the cart path, it will take you around the front field. If you want to go further, there is a path into the woods at the far end of the field. It will lead you to a small creek. Take a break in the shade if you like. You'll see a wooden bridge that will take you across the creek into an even bigger field. The path goes around the field next to the woods and ends back at the bridge. It should take you about two hours. After that, you must be back and ready to take Alex upstairs to Madam."

"Thank you, Edward. We'll see you later." Bryan started to tap Alex with the reins.

"Oh! One last thing." Edward took a large feather plume and attached it to her headstall. "Also, sir, here is a little basket of goodies for you." He handed Bryan a covered basket. "Enjoy your ride."

Bryan slapped Alex on the back. "Let's go, Alex." She started to pull the cart down the dusty path that led to the front field. He was surprised at how easily she pulled the cart, even though the path was rock hard. Had the ground been soft dirt, she would have had a hard time pulling the cart. They soon arrived at the small bridge and creek Edward had mentioned.

This was a totally new experience for Bryan: a cart ride pulled by his very own pony girl, not to mention that he was outside and just as naked as she was. "Whoa, Alex!" he called and pulled back on the reins. The bit pulled rigid in her mouth and she stopped immediately.

She had done a very good job, so it had not been necessary for him to use the whip on her ass. He was fascinated with watching her ass wiggle and her breasts bob up and down with each step she made.

It was warm and he had started to sweat some; Alex was also sweating from the exercise. He opened the basket that Edward had given him and found a bottle of Scotch, a glass, and a very unusual vibrator.

Bryan got out of the cart and loosened the bit in Alex's mouth so she was able to talk. "I want to ask you a few question, if that's okay," he said. "Take a few swallows of the Scotch." He held the glass to her mouth.

"Sir, I'm not supposed to have any of that," she said.

"It's okay, I'm not gonna tell. Take some, it'll help; it's hot out here," he replied.

"Thank you, sir. Yes, it will help a lot."

Out of the basket, he took a small towel, walked down to the water's edge and soaked the towel in the cool running water, and returned to her side. Wiped down her face and body, taking extra care with massaging her breasts, nipples, pussy, and ass.

"How did you get mixed up with the madam? Do you do this willingly?" he asked.

"Well, sir, the madam has ten very beautiful girls who stay in the house on a regular basis, and she takes very good care of all of us. We get paid very well for the things we do. I get a little extra for being a pony girl; you see, not all the girls pull carts.

"Like all the girls, I wrote to her about a job in her house. She said that she had only room for ten, but there were forty-five on a waiting list if any of our group left. She says she gets ten to fifteen letters a week from pretty girls wanting to come to the house."

"What do the other girls do, if they don't pull carts?" Bryan asked. "Madam Wong said I could do almost anything I wanted to you."

"There's one thing that only a few of the girls do that I don't want to do. Madam has not made me do it yet, but it does pay a lot more money," Alex said. "Some very rich people come to see her from time to time, and tonight I will be pulling one of them in this same cart.

"We'll go on the other side of the field deep into the woods. There's a platform that the girl is tied to. She is gagged and only her ass cheeks are exposed; everything else is protected.

"The man I will be pulling around tonight will be given a handheld mini-bow with twenty small darts. The darts have very small tips, but they are very sharp. He will stand off about ten steps and shoot the darts, ten in each ass cheek. Edward will count the number that stick in and stay and mark their position.

"Some time in the next few days, more men will come and test their skills. At the end a winner is proclaimed. All the other men then pay for him to have any of madam's ten girls. The girl who can keep still enough and take the most darts will get a very big bonus."

"Why did Edward put this vibrator in the basket?" Bryan asked, inspecting it.

"Sir, the path for the last few hundred yards to the house goes uphill and things slow down some. The vibrator helps the pony girl move along a little faster." She paused. "I know we're going around the big field now, but if you like you can put it in me anyway. It's okay."

Bryan eased one part of the double-pronged vibrator into her pussy as far as it would go. The second part, which was smaller, he inserted into her ass. She winced a little when that went in. The vibrator was attached to a leather belt that snapped to the waist belt in front, between her legs, and in the back. He then turned it on.

"I see," Bryan said. "I guess we better get going." He replaced the bit in her mouth and climbed back into the cart. Off they went.

She was right: even with the vibrator and butt plug in place, she slowed down for the last few hundred yards. Bryan gave her a cut across the ass with the whip, and she jerked and picked up her foot. His second stroke was on the other cheek; she jerked again and picked up her other foot. The third stroke did the trick. The cart jerked forward, and for the last few yards to the house, she was almost running.

"Sir." Edward smiled at seeing her moving so fast. "Did you have a nice cart ride?"

"Absolutely, Edward, I sure did. I'd like to do this again sometime."

"I'm quite sure Madam could arrange that, but for now, we must get her out of the harness and give her a bath. She must be in excellent shape when you take her back upstairs to Madam."

"Okay, Edward, I'm game. What do we do?"

"Follow me and bring her along." Edward handed the leash to Bryan after taking Alex out of the harness and removing the vibrator. "See that platform with the shower head over it? Have her stand on that and face forward."

Bryan followed his instructions and Edward turned the water on. The men watched as Alex shivered under the frigid water. After two hours of being in the hot sun, the cold water only added to her discomfort.

Bryan toweled her dry, stopping only to massage all her special body parts. When he completed his task, Edward told him to step inside the dungeon room, where he could take a shower and get dressed. He had to brush Alex's hair dry.

When this was done, it was time to start upstairs. All of a sudden Edward stopped at the dungeon door. "Mr. Wescott, sir, when you brought Alex downstairs, she was on her hands and knees. She must return to Madam the same way. Alex, I'm surprised at you for forgetting that rule. One other thing: you need to put the ball gag in her mouth as well."

"Edward," Alex said, "I'm sorry I forgot. Are you going to punish me?"

"No, not now. I'll think about it later. Maybe I'll let your next client know to give you a few minutes extra with his choice of whip so you won't forget again."

"Thank you, Edward," she said as Bryan put the gag in her mouth and buckled it. She then returned to her hands and knees.

In the study upstairs, Madam Wong sat talking to Kelly and Peggy and waiting for their arrival. "Ah! Yes, here they are now," she said and came to inspect Alex. "Dear, did you have a nice time with Mr. Wescott?" She petted Alex's head.

Alex looked at Madam Wong and nodded.

"Mr. Wescott, how about you? Did you enjoy your day with my little slave girl?"

"You truly have a treasure in this young woman; I can't begin to tell you the intoxicating pleasure I have had with her. Her willingness to achieve such a high standard to pleasure me gives me a very high regard for your establishment."

"Thank you kind sir," Madam Wong replied. "Edward, you can take her to her room for a little rest now. She has another cart ride with another client in two hours," she said. "Also, if you will, get the cart and take Judy down to the platform for tonight's activities. She needs to spend a little extra time tied to the platform."

Edward took the leash from Bryan and walked out of the room with Alex following on her hands and knees.

"If you would be so kind, I do have other business to attend to," Madam informed the group.

"Yes, Madam, thank you for today's adventure. There's a tip with the envelope for your kind efforts," Kelly said. "We must be going; I have just received a call from the office I need to attend to."

The setting sun was a red ball in the sky over the pine forest as they drove off the property. Bryan turned and waved goodbye to such an amazing day.

"That was Sara Jean on the phone, Bryan," Kelly said. "We have a meeting with the ambassador as soon as we get back."

The ambassador seemed worried when they sat down at his desk. "I just got off the telephone with Greg Jeffers. Even with all our successes of yesterday, there is still a lot of work to do, and I have more disturbing news.

"Kelly and Peggy," he continued, "you're to leave right away to fly back to the island. We researched the building with the people who leased the island to Rema, and from their records, you only found half of the house during your raid. We think there is a complete complex of hidden rooms under the main building.

"Also, we obtained further information from the furniture owner: there is another control chair down there someplace. It may lead you to those rooms. We know Ivan Ross has two of the missing women in Britain someplace, but the other four may still be on that island."

The Ambassador turned to Bryan. "You have a friend named Kim, is that correct?" he asked.

"Yes, sir, I do. Is she okay?" Bryan asked, puzzled by his question.

"Greg thinks so, but he's not sure," the Ambassador said. "She's been kidnapped, and we think it was Rema's men. Greg said she was supposed to have met with another woman, a Pat Howard, and she never showed up."

"How does he know she was kidnapped?" Bryan was anxious.

"It seems she's been missing for two days now. There was a witness who filed a police report about seeing a big black car run her car off the road into a field. Two men grabbed her, put her in the back seat, and drove off. The car she was driving was registered to Kelly.

"The lady witness could not get a plate number, but she did see a orange ball on the plate as they drove off. Greg thinks it was a Florida tag. It wasn't until yesterday that Pat called Bill and inquired about Kim; that's when they called the police and put things together.

"You're to leave first thing in the morning for an air base in south Florida, to meet with a Major James. He is a strike team leader with the Army and is working with other agents. Greg also thinks that with the information you came up with about Baltic and Rema's trip to Florida, they may be taking her there. He wants you to assist.

"Good luck all," the Ambassador said, "and good hunting."

"Well, Kelly, and my dear Peggy," Bryan said, "my lovely partners, it seems like I'm always saying goodbye to you. You watch your pretty asses now. I really wouldn't want to see anything bad happen to them, you know."

Kelly's sensuous smile turned a little wicked. "You take care of yourself as well, but I really can't believe you let Kim go see Pat."

"I was gonna be gone for too long. It was the least I could do," Bryan said, shrugging his shoulders.

Kim's New Owner (Chapter 5)

The Florida sun had dipped below the hanging Palmetto palms when Ray Darling turned on the small table light to brighten the plush living room. He made two bourbon and cola drinks, gave one to Rema, and sat down on the couch across from Rema. They had been there most of the afternoon discussing the operation and the upcoming trip.

"Mr. Rema, the sub is ready," Ray informed the balding man. "I talked with the captain this morning. He told me the sub is loaded. He would only need a few minutes to heat the engines up, and then we could get underway."

"Excuse me gentlemen." Another man entered the room.

"Yes, Lars, what is it?" Ray asked

"Sir, I just got a call from Tommy. He said his men have the young blonde and should be here in about fifteen minutes."

"Did he say if she gave him any problems?"

"He said the girl is a little witch and did fight a bit, but they calmed her down. She's better now." Lars chuckled. "Handcuffs behind her back made a huge difference."

"Lars," Rema said. "Have Tommy bring her in here when they get in. Oh, have you heard from Pete?"

"Yes sir," Lars replied. "Pete and his men picked up the girl named Kim as you requested. They had to stop at the warehouse in Atlanta to get what Ray needed, but he'll be here later this evening. He said he would call."

"Very well, Lars, thank you," Rema responded.

Since the death of Ted Darling, his younger brother Ray had picked up the slack and assisted Rema, Baltic, and Colonel Lee Suko in their kidnapping and gunrunning operation. Rema decided which women would be kidnapped, and Ray's men carried it out.

They had employed a small dredging company to increase the size of the inlet behind Rema's home, then spent a lot of time and money building a wooden cover over the canal large enough to hide Rema's submarine.

When he was closing that deal with the construction company, Colonel Suko had noticed a young and sexy administrative assistant, Janet Simmons. Suko had always wanted a young, pretty, and sexy American woman to be one of his lovely sex slaves at his mountain hideaway in North Korea. He paid Rema his going rate for her, so Ray Darling had his men kidnap the young woman for shipment to Suko's place.

Meanwhile some miles up the East Coast, Rema had another group of Ray's men find and kidnap Kim Hazelwood. Rema felt he had paid too much money for her favors at the slave auction he attended at the Club. Kim would now be his property until he got tired of her, and then he would sell her to the highest bidder or just give her to Suko. As pretty as she was, it would not be hard to find someone to take her.

There was a knock at the door. In walked Tommy with two other men behind him and the young blonde, Janet Simmons, with her hands handcuffed behind her. "Bring her in, Tommy." Rema gestured toward the front of his chair.

She shrugged her shoulders, her blond mane flowing around her face. Tommy forced her forward.

"She give you much trouble?" Rema asked, glaring at the woman with his cold black eyes.

"Yes, sir," Tommy said, "she sure did, but after a little push, shove, and those handcuffs behind her back, she settled down."

"I know you. I've seen you before," Janet said, daggers in her eyes. "What the hell am I doing here, and why'd these goons kidnap me? Damn it, get these handcuffs off me!" She tugged at her wrists.

"Dear lady." Rema smiled. "If you remember me, then you remember Colonel Suko. He's the one that bought you, and he paid me a lot of money to have you shipped to his house in North Korea."

"Yeah, I remember you," she said, thinking back to the meeting several months before. "All of you came to our company about the big dredging job, and I'm not going anywhere with you or that guy Suko. I'll rot in hell first."

"Easy, young lady," Rema said, shaking his head and adjusting himself in his chair. "I'd be a little careful if I were you about making statements like that. You might get your wish."

"Listen, you bastard," Janet said, fire in her eyes. "Take these damn handcuffs off me and let me go! I've had about enough of this!" She pulled away from Tommy. Tommy grabbed her again by the shoulders and shook her until she settled down.

"All right, my dear." Rema smiled with his wretched black eyes. "Everybody has choices in life, and you're about to have two. Now, you listen up and you listen real good." Rema's demeanor changed drastically. "This is the way it is. First off, you're gonna strip. After that, you're gonna go with Tommy to the submarine, he's gonna lock you in Ray's cabin, and you're not gonna give him any trouble.

"That's your first choice. Your second choice is, if you give Tommy any trouble, he's just gonna take that sexy naked body of yours out in the back field and shoot a few holes in you. What's left, he'll just put in the swamp for the alligators to eat. I'll just give Suko back his money or get him someone else. The choice is yours. So what's it gonna be?"

Janet was stunned. A few hours earlier she'd been on her way home from work and gotten run of the road by what she thought was some crazy driver. Darling's men had grabbed her, forced her into their car, tied her up, and brought her here.

She had tried to fight against them, but with three strong men against one woman; it was just too much to fight off. Now she was going in a submarine to North Korea to some bastard named Suko, and she had no say-so about any of it.

"Take the cuffs off." Her attitude mellowed. Taking her clothes off in front of these men was repulsive, but she knew that if she didn't, her life was over. She knew Rema meant business. "I don't want to be alligator food," she declared, a resigned frown on her face.

"I hope you and your men get an eyeful." She paused for a few seconds, then removed her clothes and threw them into a small pile on the floor. She stood before the men, naked and humiliated, as they stared at her sensuous and seductive body.

Tommy pulled her hands behind her again and secured the cuffs to her wrists. Her breasts and hard nipples jutted from her chest. Her frightening situation and labored breathing caused them to heave up and down. Something unthinkable in her life had happened: she was kidnapped, naked, and the property of a North Korean colonel.

"What about my clothes?" she asked as Tommy turned her around to leave the room.

Rema smiled. "Bring her over here, Tommy, and put her on her knees. Dear girl," he said, "you had better learn right now to keep that mouth of yours shut.

"Tommy, turn her around and make her bend forward. Pull her hands up high; that'll do it. I want that ass and pussy of hers up in the air." Rema's instructions sent a frantic shiver through Janet, especially when her face touched the floor.

"You two guys stand beside her and keep her still. I don't want her moving around much." Tommy's two men moved into place. Whack! Rema's riding crop found its mark on her ass cheek.

"*Ahee!*" Janet screamed. Rema followed with another malicious blow to the other cheek. "*Ahee!*" she screamed again. "*Damn, that hurts, you sorry bastard, that hurts!*"

More strokes followed, and her screams turned to whimpers of humiliation and despair. She was about ready to snap when he stopped the whipping. Her ass was a mess of scarlet welts and her pussy was aflame.

"Now, about your clothes," Rema said, satisfied that she had gotten his point. "You won't be wearing any for a long time. You'd better get use to it.

"Tommy, take her to the sub and chain her to Ray's bed. He can deal with her from there."

"Sir," Lars returned to the living room, stepping aside as Tommy left with Janet in tow. "I just got a call from Pete. He said he would be here with the girl in about half an hour."

"Great," Rema said, taking another swallow of his bourbon. "Tell the guys to bring her in here when they arrive, and tell the captain I want to be underway as soon as we can get her on the sub." He turned to Ray. "Ray, I think you'd better let the skipper of the *Colotta* know that we'll be on our way soon. He's got to make arrangements for us to dock with the ship. Tell him I want the sub locked up and in international waters as soon as he can get us there."

For almost two years, Tony Rema and his men had been kidnapping women all along the East Coast for some very wealthy people. These people hand-picked the women they wanted to become their sex slaves, and Rema's men made it happen. Using his ships, Rema had the ability to transport these women to their new owners. He also supplied a large number of guns to some of these same people for enormous amounts of money.

He already had a cargo ship and used it for most of his illegal operations, but he needed something else. In one of his large gun deals with Libya, he'd been able to buy an older diesel submarine.

In international waters, he and his twenty mercs could use the sub to move in and out of isolated areas. They would be undetected by authorities and he could complete the slave transfers and gun deals, most of which were done on an island off the coast of Greece.

The isolation of the island had provided a more secure place where the military could not scan for unauthorized ships, but the recent raid had eliminated that. To help combat this scanning problem, Rema had rebuilt the inside of the cargo ship. It now had a moveable floor and was big enough that the submarine could dock in the ship's belly. Any radar in the area would only detect commercial shipping and not the sub.

Pete's car pulled into the small parking lot behind the house and his men got out with Kim, her hands handcuffed behind her back. A minute or two later, they entered the living room where Rema and Ray waited.

"Ah! Kim," Rema's eerie voice broke the silence in the room. "It's about time I get to see you again. You have eluded me for too long."

She raised her head to face him. "You. I knew it had to be you. How did you find me?" she said, tingling with fear and apprehension.

"I have my ways, dear girl." He smiled. "I have my ways."

"Now that you have me, what are you gonna do with me?" she asked softly, afraid that if she showed anger, he might hurt her.

"If you remember, we had a fun-filled evening together, but I paid too much for you for the pleasure I got. That damn other guy wanted you almost as much as I did. I hope you enjoyed all that money you got from me."

"You tried to kidnap me once before, but you got Christy instead of me, if you remember," she told him.

"Yes, I know. Ted's men screwed up." Rema frowned. "I've found out that a guy named Bryan Wescott was trying to shut down my operation. Is he the one that shot Ted Darling on the ship that night? I bet you know all about what happened that night, don't you? I also found out you moved in with him and you've been his ever since. Now you belong to me. Such sweet revenge, don't you think?"

"Tell us, bitch!" Ray broke in. "I want to know who killed my brother. I want to go kill the bastard."

Kim didn't speak. Thinking she might have already said too much, she just bowed her head.

"Easy, Ray," Rema said, taking control of the conversation. "We'll find out what happened. There'll be plenty of time on the sub to find out what she knows; it's plain to see she knows more than she's telling. I might enjoy getting the information out of her myself." He looked back at Kim. "Kim, you asked what was going to happen to you. Well," he paused a few seconds, "if you remember what took place at the auction that will become almost an everyday thing for you, in one way or another."

Rema watched her with penetrating eyes, fascinated by her desperation. "Like all the others that have gone before you," he said. "Each one had a choice. Not much of one, mind you, but still a choice. Pete is gonna take off the handcuffs, and you will remove all of your clothes. You won't need them any more. If you don't do it, he'll just cut them off."

Kim knew what kind of man Rema was and how he could torture a woman. She removed her clothes, put them in a pile on the floor, and stood naked in front of the men.

"Put the cuffs on her again, Pete, behind her back. Kim, on your knees in front of me," Rema instructed.

Rema unbuckled his pants and pulled them down to expose his rock-hard cock. "You remember this don't you my dear?" He stroked it a few times. "I know you do," he said, taking in the full view of her incredible body. "What do you think, Ray? She's amazing, isn't she?"

"I must say," Ray said, admired the view, with another drink in his hand, "she's by far the most gorgeous piece of ass we've kidnapped yet. Would you look at those tits and those nipples? And man, not a hair anywhere around that slit of hers."

"Come, closer my pet," Rema said, continuing to stroke his cock. "Open your mouth. *Now*! Do it quick."

She knew she had no choice but to obey his sadistic request. She opened her mouth; he grabbed the back of her head and forced her mouth over his shaft.

Her lips closed around his massive member, and she shut her eyes. Taking a handful of hair and still holding the back of her head, he guided his cock in and almost out of her mouth. She winced from the pain when he used his other hand to cup her left breast and squeeze and pinch her nipple.

Kim thoughts raced back to Bryan. She only wished it was his cock in her mouth and not this savage sadistic bastard's. It was a strange fascination to feel Rema's cock in her mouth; she had felt it before and lived through it.

She only hoped she could live through it again. Maybe Bryan might find a way to rescue her, but he was still in London.

Soon, stimulated almost to the breaking point Rema moaned and pushed his cock forward. His body stiffened. "Sooo goood," he gasped. His explosion erupted against the back of her throat, almost gagging her as she swallowed the slippery liquid.

His orgasm finished, he pulled her head back by the hair, causing his cock to ease from her mouth. She closed her lips. "Now, my sexy little wench," he said with a crude smile on his face, "didn't that taste good? You'd better get used to it: it's gonna be a part of the menu for you."

Lars entered the room, the entertainment over. "Sir," he said, "the sub captain is ready to get underway as soon as you are. He said he talked to the captain on the cargo ship, and they're ready for you as well."

"Thanks, Lars," Rema said. "Pete, his two men, you, and Tommy's two men will stay here and clean things up a bit. Tommy will be going with us; we're gonna need his help. You're in charge until we get back. Should be about six weeks.

"I'll be calling you in the next few days about a truck shipment of high-powered rifles and ammo being sent to a military base in North Carolina. The word is it's about a thousand or so; it's a nice shipment. Pete and his men are gonna hijack the trucks and take the guns to the Atlanta warehouse. Let things settle down some and rent a couple of vans to move them to the storage building out back. I'll deal with them when we get back. My guy in Greece liked my last shipment and these have a special price on them. They got some unique laser sight that can be accurate up to almost a mile. I've been told it's like shooting fish in a barrel.

"Take Kim to Tommy on the sub and tell him to get her cleaned up and fed like the other woman. Have him chain her to my bed in my cabin. Tell the captain we'll be on board in about fifteen minutes."

"Where're we meeting the good colonel, Mr. Rema?" Ray asked.

"Just off the coast of Japan," Rema explained. "He's gonna fly in by seaplane and we're gonna transfer as much of the shipment to the plane as we can. We'll unload the rest when we get there. He's gonna stay with us on the sub to get us through Korean waters; we don't want their navy shooting us."

"The Koreans are paying us a lot of money for these weapons. I don't want to disappoint them in any way. Let's go."

The Chase (Chapter 6)

The cold clouds of London turned to the hot sun of Florida as the private Lear jet touched down on the airbase tarmac. Bryan had been in the air for about seven hours and was a little tired, but glad to be back on US soil. He was the only person on the plane except for one flight attendant and the two pilots.

The base personnel seemed to be ready for him; he watched the plane gradually come to a stop about fifty yards from an isolated hangar. The crew hurried from the hangar with a set of stairs and attached them to the plane's door.

As he was leaving the plane and thanking them for the ride, a Jeep stopped a few yards from the steps. A young woman was driving, dressed in a green camouflage army suit, with a green beret tilted on her head. "You Bryan Wescott?" she called.

"Yes, yes, that's me," he called back, holding up his left hand as he came walking down the metal stairs.

"Get in," she instructed, her voice high-pitched, "and put your bag in the back seat. I'm supposed to take you to the operations center right away; they're waiting for you. You must really be someone important, for them to be waiting on you. Even the major is a little jittery about what's been going on."

"I'm not sure about being all that important," he replied, "but I do need to see a Major James as soon as you can get me to him."

"By the way, my name's Corporal Henderson, and I've been assigned to escort you around the base as long as you're here," she said.

Bryan couldn't tell much about her figure because of the clothes, but he could tell she was young and very attractive. His mind raced back to Kelly and Peggy. He loved seeing them in their military uniforms. They didn't do much for their figures, but he knew from past experience how lovely their bodies were. She seemed to be in the same league.

The trip to the operations center only took a few minutes; he and Corporal Henderson entered the single-story building after being screened by the security guard at the door. She escorted Bryan to the conference room door. "I'll be here when you're ready to leave," she told him.

Inside the room, a man in uniform greeted him. "Glad you're here, Mr. Wescott. My name is Major James." They shook hands. "This is Gene Carter, CIA, and he's in charge of this operation. The rest of the folks here are from all branches of law enforcement in our government: FBI, CID, and a few others."

The major continued, "I'm in charge of a forty-man strike force that has been assigned to help you find this guy Rema, and maybe raid his place if we can find it. My men and women are standing by with four helicopter gun ships and we have the capacity to deal with just about anything that's out there."

"That's great," Bryan replied, wondering just how they were going to find Rema's house. "I hope we don't need all that, but I guess with Rema, you never know." He turned to Carter. "Let's see what we have so far, Mr. Carter. How do we stand?"

"Okay, folks, gather round, if you will." Carter gestured toward the conference table. "This is what we got so far," he continued. "From the intel Mr. Wescott gave us from London, we know that Baltic, Rema, Darling, and the Korean Colonel employed a dredging company to increase the size of a waterway for a ship to go directly to the ocean. We only know of a few companies around here that can do that big of a job. We have people investigating these companies as we speak.

"We received word this morning that another young woman has just been reported missing, a Janet Simmons, and yes, she works for a construction company. They told us they did a big write-up for a dredging job for Rema. We think that's where Rema came in contact with Miss Simmons.

"Mr. Wescott, of course we know about your Kim being kidnapped, and the ties with Rema. We believe that Rema is in Florida, and we want this guy. With his dealings with the North Koreans, it could get messy. Our only problem is, we don't know exactly where in Florida he is. Our satellites have taken pictures of the east and west coastlines of the Florida Everglades.

There are eight possible areas where a ship of that size can hide. We need more information before we start flying in and raiding these places."

"Gene—is it okay if I call you Gene?" Bryan asked.

"Sure, please do," Gene answered.

"The last time I talked to Greg Jeffers, he told me Ted Darling had a younger brother living near the Everglades, but no one has been able to run him down."

"That's right," Gene confirmed. "Ray Darling is his name, but we don't have much intel on him."

There was a knock on the door and a messenger came in to give Gene a report. "Listen up, folks," Gene said, addressing the group. "Our guys interviewed the owner of the dredging company Rema employed. They said their people were picked up by Rema's bus each day from a hotel and driven to the work location on the lower west tip of the state. They said the windows of the bus were painted and they couldn't see where they were going.

"All of their equipment was already there and all they had to do was go to work. They did the dredging work and build a wooden roof structure over the waterway large enough to hide a ship." Carter paused. "There are only two houses in that area that fit their description. Major, you have a recon team ready to go?"

"That's right, an eight-man team standing by," the major said.

"Probably want to split them up, one to take Alpha target and the second for Bravo target. Let me show you on the map."

The two men set their plans into motion. The teams were to move in through the edge of the Everglades just before dark, get a good look at the two places, report their findings, and not make contact with anyone.

As dusk started to settle in the western sky, Bravo team reported that they had surveyed their target and seen only an older man and a woman in the house. There was a big yacht, but nothing else even looked close to what they were looking for. The major told the team to report to the landing zone and stand by.

Several minutes later, Alpha team reported in with different information. They had counted three guards outside the big house, but there could be more inside. The backyard of the house led down to a large waterway that seemed to lead to the ocean. The waterway had a very large covering over one end of it with foliage all over and around it. It was big enough for a ship, but there wasn't one there.

The team couldn't get close to it, but they had seen a large warehouse behind and off to the right of the house.

Major James told Bravo team to join up with Alpha team and hunker down for the night, but if they encountered any changes, to let him know immediately. The plan was to raid the place at first light.

"Mr. Wescott," Major James said, "You have heard the reports. I think this is our best bet, but I don't want to start this operation at night in the Everglades. We'll be ready to hit the place at daylight.

"Corporal Henderson will see to it that you have a place to stay and something to eat. She'll have you here in the morning, ready to go."

"Thank you, Major. I'll see you then," Bryan said as he left the room.

Back in the Jeep, the corporal took Bryan to a nice restaurant for a nice meal. "Does the corporal have a first name?" he asked.

"Yes, I do," she replied, smiling, and letting her hair down. "It's Kathy. I wondered how long it would take before you asked me my first name."

"Nice name," he replied, "but what's a beautiful young woman like you doing in the military with a strike team?"

"Joined to have some adventure, I guess," she said, setting her water glass down. "I might ask you the same question?"

He thought for a second, peering into the dark eyes of this young beauty. "I moved from out west to the East for a better job. By accident, I got mixed up with this kidnapping thing. It's mushroomed from that. I met a young woman named Kim Hazelwood, we were getting along fine, and now she's been kidnapped by Rema."

"She must be a very special lady for you to do all the things you've been up to," Kathy said.

"Kim's a very unique person and does some amazingly special things for me. Not to mention, she's the prettiest woman I've ever known."

"Don't most women do special things for their men?" she asked, a little giggle in her voice.

"Yes, they do," he admitted, "but Kim, well, she's very submissive to some unusual activities I like to do."

"Unusual activities? Like what?" she asked, her eyebrows raised.

"I shouldn't be telling you this," he commented. "She loves bondage and likes to get spanked while we make love. Have you ever been spanked while you make love?" He was wondering how far she wanted to take this conversation.

Kathy almost turned over her empty water glass. "No!" she exclaimed with a grin on her face. "I haven't, but I've been told it's a very unique experience."

They left the restaurant and drove to the far end of the base, where Kathy took Bryan to a special private section of VIP housing. The place reminded Bryan of some gated estates, but there was no guard at the gate. There was a sign that read, "The Cottages." "What's this place?" he asked.

"The major told me that you were on assignment in Europe for the government and helped rescue several kidnapped women. He also told me you uncovered a large stash of weapons that a guy named Baltic was gonna sell to a criminal in Northern England. He wanted me to make sure you had a nice place to stay while you were here," she informed him.

"These are private cottages," she explained. "They are very nice and very private. The base administration uses them for special VIP visitors. I think you qualify for that. Let me show you in."

They entered one of the cottages. It was dark, but they soon found a light and illuminated the spacious living room. Bryan put his bag down and surveyed the four-room cottage. "Nice place," he said. "I'm sure I'll be comfortable here."

He sat down in the lounge chair and studied Kathy, who stood in the middle of the living room. "I've been watching you," he said softly. He could see her eyes questioning why she was there with him and what she should do next.

Eventually, she sat down on the rug and removed her boots and socks, then unbuttoned her shirt and removed it. Bryan watched the show as she finished undressing in front of him.

She smiled at him. Bryan inspected her with penetrating eyes from her neckline down her sleek athletic frame to her feet. Her breasts were on the small size, but stood firm and proud from her chest. Her nipples were hard and erect, standing like two valuable rubies.

His eyes migrated down to her pussy, where only a slight patch of hair showed around her pink mound. She kept her arms by her sides, letting him take in the view of her velvet offering.

"You're a bad little girl, aren't you?" he asked. "On your knees in front of me." His order resonated in the silent room. "Put your hands behind you." She followed his instructions without question.

She shivered slightly as he bent over her. He locked the cold metal handcuffs he retrieved from his handbag, and snapped them into place around her waiting wrists. He could feel the heat emanating form her incredible body, and her scent was intoxicating. Her eyes surveyed his lean, masculine form when he stood up and undressed in front of her. She followed his every movement as he sat down on the edge of the chair in front of her. Then she said in a voice just above a whisper, "I've never been handcuffed before."

"How does it feel?" he asked.

"Exciting," she replied, "but it's a little frightening to be so helpless."

"You've been thinking about doing something like this for a long time, haven't you?" He knew her feelings. She was almost like Kim: the submissive splendor of her soft face focused on his cock. He could feel she was desperate for a challenge to explore new sensuous avenues.

"Yes, sir," she said, like a good slave should say. "For a long time now, I've wondered what it would be like to be a helpless woman, unable to stop someone from using my body. I have a good body," she declared.

He watched her watching him stroke his hard cock, the purple head bouncing up and down. "Open your mouth now," he said. "Remember, only your lips and tongue, no teeth." Her eyes blinked once; then she swallowed once and opened her mouth. He put his left hand behind her head and eased her forward. His cock slid in, and she lightly closed her moist lips around his shaft.

"Ah!" he gasped, "that does feel so good!"

He pushed his cock forward slightly and pulled it back. She established a rhythm to match his, and the mouth fuck continued.

After several minutes of this action, Bryan knew he would unload his seed if things didn't slow down. She was to pretty for this to be finished. He stopped the action and stood up. She watched, quietly, puzzled at the turn of events but letting him take control of the scene.

Bryan released her from the handcuffs and told her to turn around, but stay on her knees. He took two short coils of cotton rope from his bag, and then tied one around each of her wrists.

"Spread your knees as wide as you can," he instructed, "and put your hands and arms between your legs." When she did so, her head was touching the floor and her ass and pussy were pushed towards the ceiling.

He tied each of her wrists to her outstretched ankles and wrapped the rope around the sole of each foot to keep her from pulling back on the rope.

She was now in a very proper position for his black riding crop that he took for his suit case. His first stroke was not hard, but enough for her to wiggle her ass some. A small red welt formed on her ass cheek that matched the whip's wide end.

The second stroke was much harder, this time to her other cheek. "*Ahee!*" she yelled as her body jerked. "*Damn!* Bry, that stings." The third and fourth strokes caused her to jerk again. Her ass globes were turning scarlet and glistening in the room's light. Bryan was having great success with this spanking.

He moved closer behind her and put his feet inside and against her ankles; this kept her legs spread wide. With his left hand he opened her slit and teased her clit, rubbing it a few times. He knew she was ready for him from the wetness of lubrication from her sex. With his right hand, he placed his rod against the opening and slowly slid his cock deep inside her.

"Ahhh!" she moaned. His hard rod explored the inner regions of her sex channel. She tried to arch her ass against him as he pounded her from behind. He continued for several minutes slowing his movements and then speeding up.

He picked up the riding crop and slashed her ass cheek with another resounding slap. At the same time, he pushed forward, deep into her sex.

"Agggg!" she whimpered. She sobbed again and again as he intensified the whipping and hammering of her pussy, with his cock.

His cock was harder now, almost ready to explode into her flesh. Bryan could feel her brace herself for what was to happen. He felt the enormous heat from her red glowing ass; he knew she was in ecstasy. He had not bargained for this. How many times had she come during the penetration; he had lost count. Now it was his time to release his seed. His body stiffened; he held his breath and exploded deep inside her canal.

Western Florida has beautiful beaches, but it also covers some very desolate country, especially around Alligator Ally that's between the east and west coast of the state. The chase was on. The strike team, Bryan, Gene, and Corporal Henderson were now landing in a field in an area close to the ocean, and north of the Everglades. Bravo team had set flares for the helicopters, with two flying in first and then the second two landing with Bryan and the crew. The strike force rendezvoused with the Alpha recon team and proceeded to the target.

In the dim dawn light Bryan could barely see the forty men and women taking fighting positions around the house. At the major's command, a group of eight battered the front door in and entered the house.

Several gunshots rang out, people yelled, and the gun battle continued. Bryan heard the radio operator's radio echo that a strike team member had taken a bullet in his leg and was down. They had killed three of the men inside.

More gunfire and another call came in: another man had left the house, shooting back as he ran down the shoreline behind the house. Strike team members were after him. Shots rang out again from outside the house; another team member took a bullet in his shoulder and was down. The shooter took several rounds in the chest from strike team members and fell dead in the backyard.

A third call came in: a sixth man had positioned himself inside the boathouse. A strike team member asked if he should take him out. Bryan exclaimed, "No! Major, we need this man alive. I know this man's got to have some information about Rema."

"Hold your fire on the guy in the boathouse. We'll be there in a minute," Major James informed his men. "We're gonna try and take this guy alive."

Bryan, Major James, Gene, and Corporal Henderson eased their way down the sloping hill behind the main house, toward the boathouse. They held a position behind some palm trees, within yelling distance of the boathouse. "Hey! In the boathouse!" Bryan yelled. "You hear me?"

"Yeah! Damn it, I hear ya," a crude voice responded.

"What's your name?" Bryan yelled again.

"Name's Pete, who're you?"

"My name is Bryan Wescott," he informed the man. "Listen, Pete, here's the deal. The strike team has killed all the folks in the house, and one of your buddies is lying dead in the yard. Another guy is about to be killed or captured in the swamp, down the shoreline. We don't want anyone else killed. Through your gun out and come out. I'll see nobody shots you."

More shoots rang out in the distance. The call came in that they had just killed the man on the beach. "You hear those shots, Pete?" Bryan yelled again. "They just killed the guy. That leaves you, so what's it gonna be? These people have enough firepower to blow up that building you're in, and they're ready to do it. Right now, I'm the only one keeping you alive. It's your choice."

The silence was deafening and lasted what seemed like minutes, although only a few seconds had passed. "Okay, okay!" Pete screamed from inside the small building. "I'm gonna throw my gun out, but you got to meet me at the boathouse. I don't want to get shot."

Kathy touched Bryan's arm, a worried look on her face. "I honestly don't think that's a smart idea, Bry," she said, a touch of firmness in her voice.

"She's right, Bryan," the Major agreed, "that's just not smart."

"I couldn't agree more," Gene chimed in. "You don't have to do this."

"Major, Gene, Corporal, I know you guy's are right. I've got to find out what this guy knows, or we'll never stop Rema and get our people back. I asked a friend of mine the same question once in a similar situation, and she said, 'It's my job.' I guess now, it's mine."

Bryan looked at them, then shouted back to Pete, "okay, Pete, but remember, if you so much as spit the wrong way, these guys might just leave enough of you for the alligators to have a snack. You got that?"

Pete threw his gun from the boathouse and Bryan stood up, extremely nervous about what he was about to do. Minutes later, Pete was walking with Bryan into the house with his hands over his head.

They handcuffed Pete and put him in a chair in front of Bryan, who was seated behind a large desk in the living room. "Where's Rema?" he asked.

"I've heard about you," Pete declared, not answering his question.

"How so?" Bryan was puzzled. He could see the sweat on Pete's forehead.

"Rema's gone. He left two nights ago, but I heard him mention your name. He said he knew you were involved with the attack on his ship by the Feds. He said you were trying to end his operation. He also said he knew the woman Kim was living with you, and the way he put it, he paid enough money for her at the auction, so he's got her."

"How did he find that out?" Bryan was really puzzled now.

"He-e-e" Pete stuttered but managed to speak. "He said he has his ways."

"Tell me more."

"He told Ray that taking this Kim woman was sweet revenge after what you did. Anyway, he left on the sub with Tommy, Ray, and the two women."

Bryan knew the chase was on now and he was getting close. He needed more. "There's been no sub activity in this part of the ocean around Florida. We've got records on that," he informed Pete. "Are you lying to me?"

More sweat poured from Pete's forehead. "No, s-sir!" he stuttered again, squirming in his chair. "I *swear*, I'm not lying, I *swear*. The sub doesn't go underwater; it stays on top most of the time. Ya see, the sub meets up with the *Colletta* about two miles out.

"Rema had a movable false bottom built in the cargo ship, big enough to house the sub. Anybody with radar or stuff can only see commercial traffic: that's how he can get in and get out. At night, running on top, it's just another ship. When the sub is not in the belly of the ship, they can move the floor and cargo back in place, and nobody can see the difference."

"Okay, Pete." Bryan's face softened a bit. "You're saving your life now. Where are they going?" Bryan held his breath, but not enough to let Pete know how important the question was. He hoped he knew more.

"Rema's gonna kill me for telling you what I've already said," Pete said, adjusting himself in the chair.

"I'll kill you right now if you don't tell me the truth," Bryan said. "Damn it! Corporal, give me your handgun."

"Bry, you sure you want to kill him?" Kathy replied.

"Okay, okay," Pete broke in, "I get the picture, just hold on. They're gonna meet up with Colonel Suko in a few weeks in the Sea of Japan. The *Colletta* will make port in Japan and unload its cargo. Rema and the sub will go to North Korea and unload the shipment he's sold to Suko and the North Koreans."

"One last question." Bryan's heart skipped a beat when he asked. "What about the women?"

"Well—" Pete seemed reluctant to continue. "I don't think I should tell you any more."

Bryan surprised everyone, including Pete, who just looked scared to death. He took the .45 handgun that Kathy had given him and cocked the hammer. He pointed the gun directly at Pete's face. "Listen up, and you listen good! I saved your life a few minutes ago. If you don't tell me the truth, I'm gonna end this right now. You got that?"

"I understand," Pete said. Bryan's words had gotten the message across; Pete was shaking as if he'd just stepped out of a freezer. "The blond woman named Janet—Suko paid Rema a lot of money for her. She's now locked up in Ray's cabin on the sub. It might be a long trip for her, knowing Ray.

"Rema whipped the hell out of her in this living room—she's a little bitch, if you ask me. Suko said he wanted a young, pretty, American blonde girl with some spirit to add to his group of sex slaves. They planned to take her to his place in the mountains, somewhere in North Korea. Honestly, I don't know where that is."

"What about the other woman, the one named Kim?" Bryan asked.

"I took her myself to Rema's cabin after he made her put on one hell of a show. He made her give him one of the best blowjobs I've ever seen, right here in front of all of us. She does a really good job of sucking dick.

"After that was over, he wanted her to tell him what happened to Ray's brother Ted. She didn't say anything, but Rema told us that she knew more about what happened and he would have a hell of a good time for the rest of the trip trying to find out more."

Janet's and Kim's Torment (Chapter 7)

Ray had spent most of his waking hours for the first few days at sea putting the ship in order. His main focus was making preparations for the delivery of the weapons shipment to Suko. Now that things were easier, he had some time to spend with his new roommate, Janet.

She was hanging on by a slender thread, locked to a bed rail by a chain attached to a metal collar bolted around her lovely neck. She hated the chain and every time she moved it would rattle, but it was long enough for her to get to the head.

Ray was with her now. He forced her to the middle of the room and made her bend over the table and spread her legs. She turned her head to one side when he forced her to put her cheek on the table, her blond hair covering her face. He put her arms behind her back and snapped a pair of metal handcuffs on her wrists. Her nerves were on edge, her heart fluttering as she thought about what this maniac might do to her.

He tied a short length of cotton rope around each of her ankles and attached each to a leg on the table. With more rope, he attached one end around the chain of the handcuffs and pulled her arms up high over her head. He attached the other end to the top rail on the bed.

"*Agggg*!" she screamed, "the cuffs are cutting my wrists in half! Please, I beg you, please loosen the rope! Please, you're pulling my shoulders out of their sockets!"

"Shut up, bitch!" he answered angrily, leaning forward and licking her jaw. "You were a bitch at the house and I'm gonna see what I can do about that. I call it attitude adjustment."

In her bent and restrained position, her ass and pussy opened to display her sex, glistening in the dim light. He rubbed her round cheeks and then sadistically squeezed the tender flesh. Her body tensed at the torturous grip, she wondered how she could stop this madman.

Ray stepped back from her, whirled his two-pronged leather whip in the air, and ripped a stroke across her right ass cheek. "*Ahee!*" she screamed in desperate pain, her body jerking against the table. A second strike to her left cheek was just as hard as the first strike. "*Ahee!*" she screamed again, this time coughing from the scream. "Please, sir, *no* more, I can't take any more," she pleaded. "I'll do anything you want." She closed her eyes and gritted her teeth.

Ray said nothing but delivered another punishing blow to her ass. Scarlet lines crossed her ass globes as he continued his savage attack. Her screams turned to low whimpers. The whipping seemed to go on forever.

The cabin phone rang, and Ray put the whip down to answer it. "Yes, Captain," he said. "I'll see the engineer right away." He hung up the phone and turned back to Janet. "You're in luck, bitch. I got an engine problem, so don't you go anywhere. I'll be back and we can finish this later."

"You're not gonna leave me like this, are you?" she begged. "Please let me go. I'll be here when you get back. I can't go anywhere. I'd be very grateful if you'd release me."

"Silly bitch," he replied, an evil grin on his face. "You're exactly where I want you. It won't hurt you to suffer for a while. You need it, anyway."

Kim could see that she was in for the long haul with Rema, although he had not done anything to her since they boarded the sub. The metal collar around her neck was bad enough, but the chain locking her to the bed was a bit much. With the cabin door locked, she was not going anywhere, but she could move around the cabin some. At least there was enough slack in the chain, that she could use the small bathroom.

Rema left the cabin early that morning and didn't return until later in the afternoon. When he did, he was in a fit of rage. She had been able to talk to him a little, but she was afraid to do too much. She knew how sadistic he was, and she knew he really might hurt her.

"Let's go for a walk," he said. "I think you need to get out of this cabin for a while. I want to talk to you anyway."

Kim felt totally helpless, naked with a metal collar locked around her neck. Now, he was going to parade her naked body around the ship in front of the crew.

He snapped a chain lead line to her collar and handcuffed her hands in front of her. "You know, I can't go anywhere, why do you have to do that?" she asked.

"Dear lady," he began, "you now belong to me and I can do anything I want to you. I want you restrained all the time, in one way or the other. It makes me so damn hard when I see you like this.

"The cuffs in front will give you a little freedom while you climb the steps in the ship. The collar—I just love pulling your lovely neck, and I know you just love it too," he explained. "I know you were a volunteer at the auction, and to do that, you have to love the pleasurable agony of torture. When I saw you tied and on display for all of us, I just needed that lovely body of yours," he told her.

They passed several members of the crew as they did their daily jobs; some took a good look, but they said nothing. Kim was glad no one said anything. She was humiliated enough as it was. She knew what they must have been thinking, but really didn't care.

Walking through the small corridors of the ship was difficult at best, but soon they were out on the deck in the fresh air. Rema stopped at the side rail, a strange, haunting expression on his face. Kim stood beside him, looking at the ocean swirling around the front of the ship and feeling the salt spray in her face.

"Why do you do the things you do?" she asked, raising her voice over the noise of the ship's engine.

"Interesting question, my dear," he said. "I guess I just love the money and the power. Selling guns can be very profitable, you know. Kidnapping selected women is a lot of fun, and as you know, I'm a torturous sadistic bastard, but so are the people I deal with." He paused and looked at her. "Now let's get down to brass tacks," he said. "I want to know all you know about what happened to Ted Darling and the men who were with him that night on the ship. Don't leave anything out—remember, while you're on this boat, it's escape-proof. The only place you could go is the middle of the ocean, and I don't think you really want that."

"Well," she said, thinking that if she didn't tell him something, he might throw her in the ocean. That was not what she wanted. A whipping and screwing by him was much more appealing than trying to swim for it. "I really don't know much," she said. "I wasn't informed of what took place until later. What I do know is that two women agents were investigating the kidnappings. Your guy Darling tried to kidnap me, but got Christy instead. We do look alike. They saw Christy's kidnapping and followed Ted's men to the warehouse, and then to the ship. The marshals raided it, and during the gun battle, I guess he got shot by an agent."

"Why didn't you tell me this at the house?" Rema's solemn voice echoed above the ocean breeze.

She shrugged her shoulders. "It's very hard to talk with a dick in your mouth, and that's where yours was for most of the time. You do remember that, I'm sure?"

Rema didn't speak, but led her back toward the sub. Ray walked up, wiping his hands on a rag. "Mr. Rema, the ship will be delayed a few hours, one of the engines messed up a bearing. Did she tell you anything about Ted?"

"Yeah, she did," Rema said, looking at him. "Ted was stupid—his men got the wrong woman. They followed them to the warehouse and then the ship. Some agent in the gun battle shot him."

After they returned to his cabin, Rema told her that even though his dick had been in her mouth for a period of time, she'd still had a chance to tell him what he wanted to know. "Dear Kim," he said, releasing her from the handcuffs, turning her around, and forcing her wrists to the metal posts of the bunk bed, "you must learn to find a way to tell me everything you know at any given time, and this little whipping scene will remind you of that."

He took a short length of cotton rope, wound the rope around her left wrist, and secured it to the bedpost at the head of the bed, and did the same with her right wrist and the back bedpost.

He tied her ankles to the bottom of the bedposts in a similar fashion, leaving her in a spread-eagle position with her back and ass exposed to his whip.

"My dear lady, you do have such a gorgeous ass, it's almost a pity to see it whipped. You must remember, though, I'm such a sadistic bastard. Passing up a chance to whip your ass is just out of the question," he explained.

"Please, sir! You don't have to whip me, I'll tell you all I know! Please!" Her pleas fell on deaf ears.

Rema put his arms around her body, cupped both of her breasts, and squeezed them as if they were large sponge balls. The massage lasted a long time, but ended with a savage pinch to each hard nipple.

"*Ahee!*" she screamed, shaking her head at the vulgar intrusion on her nipples. He continued to pinch, then release, and pinch again. "*Ahee!*" again she screamed, desperately trying to find a way to fight the fiery pain that was shooting through her bosom.

"You must never disobey me, ever," he whispered in her ear. He licked the inside of her sweet ear, then nibbled on her earlobe. "You're an incredible piece of ass. I know how much you love being totally helpless. You're my property now and forever, so you'd better get used to this."

He stepped back, picked up his four-foot single tail whip, and slashed it across her ass.

"*No*! Ahee!" she squealed. "Please, sir, please, I'm afraid you'll hurt me!" she pleaded, clenching her fists.

Her body writhed at the fiery sting on her ass—she jerked away from the whip, causing her head to sink into the mattress of the top bunk. Another slash to her backside, and more searing pain electrified her body. Rema was like a madman with his torturous whip, leaving very little of her back, ass, and legs unmarked.

Kim was beyond her limits now; she had never been whipped this hard, even when she and Bryan had their sessions together. She could only hope she would live through what Rema did to her. Maybe one day, she would be in Bryan's arms again. That seemed to be her only way of dealing with the savage attack by Rema.

Rema's cabin phone rang, interrupting his assault on her tormented body; he put the whip down and wiped the sweat from his forehead. Whipping a woman can take a lot out of you. "Yes, Captain, what the hell is it? I'm in the middle of something here. I just don't want to leave." He was silent for a few seconds. "Okay, okay, I'll be right there."

"It looks like our little session will have to be put off for a few minutes, sweetheart," Rema told Kim, wiping more sweat off his face with a hand towel. "The captain says I got a communication in the radio room and I really need to look at it." He lightly patted her ass. "You like that, don't you? I don't suppose you'll mind if I leave for a little while, do you?" he chuckled. "When I get back, I want to see how strong those nipples of yours are. Should be fun."

Shortly Rema joined Ray in the radio room; Ray was reading a telegram in his hand. "Damn it, Rema, some son-of-a-bitch got Pete and the boys at the house. This is a message from Pete's lawyer."

"Let me see that!" Rema grabbed the paper and started to read. As he did, his attitude changed to one of pure anguish. The telegram read: "Stop: Contacted you ASAP, after talking to Pete. Stop: Strike team raided house, Pete was captured, and all others killed. Stop: Agents aware of sub, the ship, and destination. Stop: Pete said man named Bryan Wescott in charge of strike."

Rema sat down in the small swivel chair next to the radio operator and looked at Ray. "This really does change things. Can't this tub go any faster? We need to let Suko know, we have a problem," he said. "We can't be caught in open sea like this.

"Contact Colonel Suko," he told the operator. "Tell him to meet us two days in advance of our scheduled meeting. Tell him to use the larger seaplane and bring a couple of his people along. We're gonna need them to help transfer some of the cargo from the sub to the plane." He turned back to Ray. "Ray, I want to try to put as much in the seaplane as we can. If we get caught up in something, at least they'll get some of their merchandise. What about that bitch you got in your cabin? what kind of condition is she in? We're gonna have to give her to Suko much earlier than we expected, and I want to be able to give him something that isn't too messed up."

"Her ass and back are marked up a bit," Ray said, "but in a few days, she'll be as good as new. Heck, I was just getting used to whipping her ass. I guess I'll just have to settle for a blowjob a couple times a day while she's still chained up."

"That's fine, just get her cleaned up and stop by my cabin. I'm gonna have another talk with Kim about this guy Wescott. I want to see if she knows something else about this pain in the ass. You might find it interesting."

Rema returned to his cabin, where Kim was still standing spread-eagled against the bunk bed, her head on the mattress. He released her, turned her around, and had her face forward, then retied her to the bedposts in the same spread-eagle position. Ray joined them.

"You take care of the bitch?" Rema asked him.

"Yeah, I released her," Ray replied. "I got one of the crew to watch her while she takes a shower. He's gonna put the collar back on her when she finishes and chain her back to the bed. She's in better shape than I thought—she'll be fine for Suko when he gets her."

Kim watched the two sadists standing in front of her and tried to imagine what they were thinking. She soon found out. "This guy of yours, Bryan Wescott, he's become a real pain in the ass," Rema blurted out. "He and a bunch of agents raided my house in Florida and killed everybody except

Pete. Damn it! We paid a lot of money getting that place fixed up like we wanted it. That son-of-a-bitch Wescott just stormed in and took it over."

He leaned over, putting his face only inches from Kim's, spit and fire in his eyes. "Who's he work for? CIA? Who?"

Kim could smell his bourbon breath. She knew he could become a madman at any second and take it out on her. "Bryan just works as a financial consultant for a company not far from where I was kidnapped." Her words were soft, almost pleading with him not to hurt her for what Bryan had done.

"You'd better tell me all of it. You know what I'll do to you if you don't. How far can you swim with your hands and feet tied?"

"You already know I'm living with him." Kim's voice trembled as she spoke.

"What else? No wait a minute," Rema said. "Ray, untie her ankles. "Okay, now pull her left ankle up and tie it to her wrist. I'll do the same with her right ankle." This left Kim suspended by her wrists and ankles with her pussy spread wide open.

Rema lightly rubbed her pussy with his wide-end riding crop. She couldn't keep her eyes off his cold, steely, frightening face. Kim swallowed hard. She knew he was going to whip her pussy. Not that that hadn't happened before, but not under these circumstances.

"I'll tell you all I know," she pleaded, "please don't—." She could not finish what she wanted to say. The first vicious strike caught her clit full force; her eyes wide open in hysterics, she tried to scream but nothing came out. Another calculated blistering strike, and then another, to her tormented pussy.

He hesitated just a bit to see if she would say anything, and she gasped, "He—he saw you with me at the auction that night."

Rema stopped the whipping and looked at her, glaring intently into her melancholy face. "I didn't see him and I knew everyone there."

"He was one of the observers that night." Kim calmed down as she spoke.

Rema listened to her explanation, the whip in his right hand, lightly tapping his other hand. "You know, taking you has taken on a new meaning." He paused. "Ted was investing three mil for me, and he used a consultant firm. I saw his name on some of the paperwork he sent for me to fill out. I bet that guy got my three mil when they raided the ship, and now I got his woman! Ain't that something? It sure is sweet revenge."

Ray broke in. "What about my brother, bitch? Did this Wescott kill him or not?"

Kim was having a difficult time hanging by her wrists and ankles against the bed, but she was able to answer his question. "*No*! He didn't, but his boss did. Bill Majors shot Ted just before he was gonna kill Bryan. At least that's what I was told."

"Please, sir," she pleaded, "I did you no wrong. I had no control over anything that happened. Please don't whip me any more. I can't stand any more on my pussy today. Can't you wait until tomorrow?"

Ray picked up a single-tale whip and flipped it in the air, slapping the table with it. The violent sound echoed loudly in the room, causing Kim to shiver uncontrollably. The next flip of the whip caught her right breast, sending a torturous sting through her chest. "*Nooo*! *Ugh*!" her scream pierced the silence in the room.

"Hold up, Ray," Rema said. "I got something else I'm gonna do. I told my lovely little slut bitch here not to hold anything back, and just like all bitches, she's got a mind of her own. I told her some of the consequences," he informed Ray. "Earlier, I told her that I wanted to see how strong her breasts were. Well, we're gonna find out." He lifted her chin with his forefinger. "You see these fishhooks?" He showed them to her.

Kim's eyes turned to stone. Her body hurt so bad, how could she take more from this madman? "I've told you everything," she pleaded.

"I know," he replied. "Ray, hold her right breast." Rema pinched her nipple to make sure it was good and hard. She winced at the burn and tossed her head to one side.

"Now Kim, what we're gonna do here is take this fishhook and pierce that nipple of yours," he said, seemingly unconcerned as to whether she liked it or not.

"*No! You can't do that! No!*"

"I will if I want to," he replied.

The barbed hook pricked her nipple; she winced in severe pain as he pushed it through the skin and it came out the other side.

"*Naaaa! Naaaa!*" she screamed, her eyes wide open, glazed in fear. Never had she experienced such agonizing pain.

Moments later, Rema completed his task by putting the second hook through her left nipple. Again, she screamed from the unrelenting pain. She hung there with her fists clenched, her breathing short. She was a nervous wreck.

"Last but not least, dear Kim, I have these two banana weights, and I'm gonna hang one on each nipple, at the end of the fishhooks. That's gonna pull those nipples down about as far as they can go."

"*Youuuu crazzzzzzy! Noooo!*" Kim saw him let go of the weights and watched her nipples dip towards the floor. Her head dropped. Her hair falling aimlessly across her chest, and her body slumped forward.

"Would you look at that, Ray?" Rema said, "I guess she's had enough. She can't feel anything more. I'm just gonna let her stay like this for a while. Oh! One more thing." He took the riding crop, inserted the handle into her vagina as far as it would go. "When she wakes up and sees that thing in her, maybe, she'll get the message."

The Stewardesses (Chapter 8)

Bryan returned to the base with the strike team, leaving the other military personnel at Rema's house. Their job was to take control of the weapons and materials that Rema had left behind. When Bryan entered the operations center, Bill Majors and Greg Jeffers met him at the conference room.

Their meeting lasted quite some time as they reviewed all the intelligence and discussed the contingency plans to capture Rema and his men. They knew Rema was to meet Colonel Suko in the Sea of Japan, and they expected the transfer of weapons to the North Koreans at the same time.

Bryan asked Bill if he had contacted Mr. Ling in Japan about his granddaughter. Bill said that he had, and that Mr. Ling was truly thankful for his help.

Bryan recounted what Mr. Ling's granddaughter had said: "Baltic bought Mr. Ling's granddaughter after seeing her at a place called Mama Sandju's Pleasure Palace. Rema's men kidnapped her when she left the building a few days later. I don't think it would be a surprise if at some point during their voyage, Rema and his men made another trip there."

"You could be right," Bill agreed. "What do you have in mind, Bryan?"

"Sir, with your approval, I'd like to visit that place and see if the owner knows anything about Rema and where he might be. Also, I think Mr. Ling might be able to help us out. I'm sure he knows the place."

Mr. Jeffers interrupted. "I think that's a good idea. Bryan, you're getting closer to that bastard, and he knows it. We don't know how many more people are involved in this thing. We do know about the hijacking that they had planned for those guns going to North Carolina. We know that there may be more hijackings planned," he concluded.

"They might have someone tracking you as well. I think that if you travel by commercial air, it might help your cover. You'll be able to blend in better with the locals. Major James and his strike team are gonna find that ship. He'll be in touch with you when you get to Japan. Good hunting."

The first part of Bryan's flight took him to Hawaii, where he made a flight change to Japan. His first-class seat was fabulous, and the special treatment was impressive. He only hoped the second part of the trip went as well as the first.

Her name was Carmen, by the nametag she wore. She was a beautiful and charming stewardess who was in charge of the first-class section. Her elegant bright smile helped put the few people in the section at ease.

He watched her as she moved from passenger to passenger, offering them food and drink, which they gladly accepted. Her professional demeanor fit just as nicely as the uniform tailored to her lean, athletic body. The small apron covered her short skirt, but did not keep Bryan from a pleasant view of a pair of sensuous legs. His thoughts were lost in imagining how she would look with only that apron on.

After the dinner and the clean-up procedures, she stopped at his seat and whispered in his ear, "would you like a drink from the bar?"

He looked into an amazing pair of captivating bedroom eyes. "Bourbon and cola would be just fine," he answered.

She smiled and touched his shoulder. "I'll be right back." A few minutes passed before she returned, but when she did, she had his drink and a soft drink for herself. "I have a little break time coming. May I join you for a few minutes?"

"Please, by all means," he replied. He took the drink and gestured for her to sit beside him. "I see your name is Carmen Parks, flight attendant."

"That's right, nice to meet you," she said.

"My compliments go to the chef on the lobster. It was a great meal," Bryan said. "I didn't expect such a meal on a plane."

"We try to do it up right in first class, you know, but I'm not the cook. Oh! Here she is now. Cindy, sit down, we got a few minutes. Mr. Wescott says he liked your lobster."

"Thank you, sir," Cindy replied. "I've had a lot of practice," she added.

"Do you have business in Japan, or is this a vacation trip?" Carmen asked.

"It's business," he replied. "I'm in search of someone. What about you ladies? You go traveling around to all these foreign places."

"Cindy and I just started this schedule to Japan. We wanted to see some new, amazing, mysterious places, and maybe meet some interesting people. You wouldn't happen to know of any places in Japan like that, would you?" she asked.

"That's an interesting question. I might, but exactly what are you looking to do?" he asked. He was wondering where the conversation was headed.

Carmen shrugged her shoulders. "Oh, I guess, something mysterious, very erotic, and daring."

Bryan hesitated. "I don't know if you're interested in it or not, but the Japanese do a splendid job in rope bondage. I understand there are several clubs downtown that accommodate erotic fantasies of this type."

"Sounds like you've had some experience in such things." She smiled, amused at his answer.

Bryan could tell she was interested by the way she was testing the waters. "Some," he said. "Not in Japan, only in the States. I'm staying in the hotel with the big 'H' on it. If you'd like to further your education in such matters, I'd love to give you a demonstration?"

"Come on, Carmen," Cindy touched her arm. "We've got to get back to work."

"I'll think about what you suggested, Mr. Wescott," Carmen said as she and Cindy moved up the aisle.

"I can't believe you, Carmen," Cindy declared. "Talking about such things like that, and with a total stranger."

"Well, for gosh-sakes, that's what our plan was, right?" she said. "Anyway, it was a good way to make contact."

Mr. Ling was true to his word. When Bryan entered the airport lobby, a driver was there to meet him and take him to his hotel. "Mr. Wescott, sir," the driver said, helping Bryan with his luggage. "Mr. Ling said your meeting with Mama Sandju is at four tomorrow afternoon. We'll pick you up in front on the hotel at three."

Bryan relaxed on the soft hotel bed for just a short time, wondering about the two lovely stewardesses he had met on the plane. Would they really stop by? He then decided a drink was in order from the downstairs hotel bar.

At the bar, he took his drink from the bartender and turned around. To his surprise, the two stewardesses from the plane were in a corner booth. "May I join you lovely ladies?" he asked, holding his glass up to toast them. They were wearing some incredibly revealing clothing, much different than on the plane.

Soon the three adjourned from the bar and headed for Bryan's room. As they entered the room, Carmen turned to Bryan. "Okay, Bryan, what's all this education you're supposed to give me?"

"To experience the full treatment," he said, "you'll have to go to one of those clubs I told you about. For now, I'll try and give you a crash course in being tied up. So, if you will, please remove all of your clothes."

The sudden request sent a shiver of excitement through Carmen's body. This was something different and totally unexpected. She had never been tied before, but always wondered what it would be like. She and Cindy had come to Japan for an adventure, and this might be a good place to start.

She unbuttoned her shirt, revealing that she had no bra on. It took only seconds before she stood before Bryan and Cindy totally nude. Cindy was surprised at how easily Carmen had followed Bryan's instructions. She knew they wanted to play, but this was way too fast.

Bryan surveyed her artistic body: she stood lean and strong with only a slight amount of pubic hair to offset her glistening slit. Carmen's hand-sized breasts and hard nipples stood strong. They invited adventurous cruelty.

"Get on your knees and put your hands behind you." He gestured toward the carpeted floor.

Carmen's long auburn hair flowed over her chest like spun silk when she eased herself to her knees. She moved with the grace of a goddess. It was an impressive sight. "Like this?" she asked, blushing while she made the move.

"That's right. Now put your hands behind your back and cross your wrist." She rubbed her hands together and completed the task Bryan had given her.

He gathered her hair and pulled it behind her head. "Let's not cover those stunning breasts of yours," he said. "Cindy, would you be so kind as to take this rope he took from his suitcase? Now, wrap the rope around her wrists."

Cindy was shocked that he had asked her for help with her friend, but she twisted the rope as he said.

"Now, bring the rope back between her wrists and cinch it together." Bryan was in complete control. The wrist tying done, he pulled out another rope from his case. "Okay, Cindy, wrap this rope around her wrists just above the other rope, and proceed up her arms to her elbows. Then take a turn between her elbows and cinch it together with two knots. It should be skin-tight." He turned to Carmen. "Carmen, how do you feel now?" he asked, fascinated at how easily she accepted the tight ropes.

"It's tighter than I expected," she replied. "But the helpless feeling I'm getting is something else." She shivered as Cindy finished the last knot.

"Cindy, "take this smaller rope." He handed it to her. "Wrap it around her ankles a few times, and then go between her ankles and cinch it together.

With the excess, secure it to her wrist. That's it, make it tight," he told her as he watched her progress.

She finished securing Carmen's ankles to her wrists and stood up with her hands on her shoulders. "How's that?" she asked with a satisfied smile.

Bryan didn't say anything—he just started to remove his clothes. Both women watched intently as he proudly displayed his masculine body. His cock was already rock-hard and stood at attention like a soldier in a parade, only inches in front of Carmen's face. "Hold her head steady, Cindy," he said. "Carmen, open your mouth. I know this is not Japanese rope bondage, but this will give you some idea of what you might be in for. No teeth now, just your lips and tongue."

Cindy had a devilish smile on her face when she held Carmen's head. She knew that this was not what either of them had expected when they talked on the plane, but they had wanted to expand their knowledge of the unusual.

Carmen blinked her eyes at his erection and tugged on the ropes that held her helpless. She knew that there was no escape—not that she really wanted to escape—but tested the tightness anyway. She was going to have to take his cock in her mouth, and there was nothing she could do to stop it: that was the thrilling part. She surrendered to her situation and opened her mouth. Bryan put his cock into her open mouth, and she closed her sensuous lips around his shaft.

The penetration was slow and deep enough that her nose touched his stomach. He started to work his cock in and out slowly, enjoying the wet heat from her mouth, but focused on the extreme softness of her rigid tongue against the underside of his shaft.

"Hold her head tight, Cindy," he said. He was breathing deeper now as he continued the artful process. Soon, he began to feel the familiar tingling building in his loins, but he was not ready for that just yet. He had other things he wanted to do to this gorgeous creature. He removed his cock slowly from her mouth.

She closed her mouth and looked at him like a lost child, almost frightened she had done something wrong. "Absolutely amazing," he said, smiling at her. "We'll get back to doing this again in a little while, but I think we need to expand things a bit.

"Grab her ankles, Cindy. I've got her shoulders. Pick her up and lay her on the bed."

Their task done. Cindy lay down face to face with the tied Carmen. "I've got you right where I want you," Cindy whispered, the devilish smile appearing on her face again. "I've wanted your cute little ass like this for a long time."

Bryan stood back and watched her, surprised by how demanding Cindy was. Carmen didn't speak; she closed her eyes and just turned some in the bed. Cindy put her arms around Carmen's shoulders, pulled her close, and lightly kissed her on her lips. Carmen returned the kiss, and smiled at her when the kiss ended.

Just like Carmen, Cindy was wearing no bra or panties. She immediately removed her clothes, and now naked, lay again on the bed beside Carmen. Bryan, still watching, was fascinated with the incredible sight of these two exquisite naked women lying on the bed and kissing each other.

Cindy's hands roamed across Carmen's body and stopped at her left breast, then started to massage the luscious firm flesh. "*Oh! That's so good,* Cindy, *please don't stop.*" Her voice quivered. Carmen's body was aflame with desire.

Cindy continued the massage, and in an instant pinched her nipple. "*Ahee!*" Carmen squealed at the torturous tweak, closing her eyes and trembling from the burn in her breast. Cindy immediately kissed her a third time, but now their tongues met and started to play with each other.

Bryan picked up his riding crop and struck Carmen's exposed left ass cheek. *Whack*! The wicked sound echoed in the silent room.

"*Agggg!*" Carmen blurted out, interrupting the kiss. Her body jerked at the cut of the whip, causing Cindy to jerk away from her sweet sensuous lips. Immediately, Cindy grabbed Carmen's shoulders, pulled her face to hers, and kissed her again. This time she held her tight enough that Bryan's second stroke did not dislodge her from the kiss.

Bryan continued with more strokes to both of Carmen's now-scarlet ass cheeks. He was about to stop and watch the two women jerking around on the bed when Carmen spoke. "Please, Bryan, don't stop, please, more, I'm about to come!" she pleaded.

The next strokes were more sadistic than before, just as hard as he would have hit Kim. As Bryan started to deliver another stroke, Carmen turned on the bed, forcing Cindy to her right. This time the whip came down on Cindy's exposed ass cheek instead. *Whack*! "Ahee!" she spit out; her body stiffened and she hugged Carmen tighter than before.

Again and again the whip found its mark on Cindy's ass. Each time she wiggled and held onto Carmen for more. Her ass was a deep red, just like Carmen's. With the women hugging each other, Bryan's whip, and the struggle in the bed, Cindy cried, "I'm coming!"

"Me too! Cindy, me too!" Carmen echoed.

Bryan stopped and watched both women stiffen, Cindy holding on tightly to Carmen as they each exploded into their own orgasm almost at the same instant. It was as if they were in slow motion, suspended in time. Reality wasn't going to come back for a while.

Bryan grabbed his cock and started to stroke it for all he was worth. He joined the women on the bed, putting his cock only inches from the mouths of both women. Cindy wrapped her soft, delicate hand around Bryan's cock. "Open your mouth, Carmen," she directed.

Carmen obediently took the purple head into her mouth and slowly closed her lips tightly around his shaft. Cindy worked his cock in and out of Carmen's mouth, making sure it stayed in place.

Bryan was elated by the penetration and the incredible feeling of Carmen's soft, hot, wet mouth against his cock. Cindy's velvet hand massaged his balls, and then she lightly pinched the skin. "Ugh!" he groaned and his member exploded its dose of nectar deep into her throat.

Bryan thought she was going to swallow his manhood, the way she was sucking it. Soon, though, she eased her grip, and the exhausted Bryan slid his cock from her mouth. Cindy immediately grabbed it and guided it into her own mouth to lick off the remaining cum.

Mama Sandju's Pleasure Palace (Chapter 9)

Bryan was impressed at how Mr. Ling's driver maneuvered the luxurious black car through the minuscule back alleys and diminutive streets of Japan. What was more impressive was that he didn't hit anyone, even though the vicinity was so crammed with people. Everyone seemed to be in a rush, but going nowhere. Mr. Ling was seated across from Bryan and Bruce Cane, the US director of legal operations for Japan.

The chauffeur stopped the car between two large deserted rustic brick buildings. The only difference between the buildings was that the one on the right side of the shabby alley had a rusty metal door. "Mr. Ling?" Bryan asked, somewhat apprehensive at the questionable surroundings. "You're sure we're in the right place? These buildings just don't look too safe, you know?"

"Mister Bryan, building on left for sale, man want lot money," Mr. Ling replied. "Mama Sandju want to buy, but man want sell for less money. Mama can't pay. Don't worry, Mister Bryan, you're in my town now." He chuckled.

Mr. Ling told the driver to wait until they returned and then pushed the small white button beside the metal door. A minute passed; then, the squeaky door opened. The man on the other side was tall and lean; a stately man, dressed in a prim and proper blue suit with a white shirt and tie. "Ah! Mr. Ling," he said in a strong oriental accent, but his English was very articulate. "Please come in. Mama Sandju is expecting you and your guests."

"Thank you, Rudy," Mr. Ling said. "Gentlemen." He turned to Bryan and Bruce. "This is Rudy, Mama Sandju's right hand. Rudy, this is Bryan Wescott and Bruce Cane."

The man's eyes focused on them. "Nice to meet you," he replied. "If you will, gentlemen, please follow me." Rudy gestured towards a small darkened hall behind him. A small and very dim light at the other end of the hall offered only enough light to guide them. The hall emptied into a large pleasant room, filled with elegant-looking lounge chairs. Several men sat talking in idle conversation; some were laughing, while others sat calm and expressionless. When Rudy and the men entered, they paid no attention to them.

"This is our waiting room, Mr. Wescott," Rudy said. He noticed how interested Bryan seemed. "The lady sitting at the table, with the computer, takes the customer's fee and arranges the time for them to see one of the ladies."

"Interesting," Bryan replied. But what was more pleasing to his eye was that the young Japanese lady was topless and sporting a beautiful set of breasts, with stunning nipples. Standing beside her with his arms folded was a large oriental man dressed in a blue suit similar to Rudy's.

"The man is our security guard," Rudy said. "Please, gentlemen, follow me upstairs. Mama Sandju is in her office." Rudy lightly knocked on the door and said something in Japanese that Bryan didn't understand. A second later, the door opened.

A beautiful young Japanese woman who Bryan suspected to be in her early twenties, stepped into the middle of the room and smiled at the men. "Mr. Ling, nice to see you again," she said. "Mr. Wescott, Mr. Cane, my name is Niki. Mama Sandju will be with you in just a minute. Please be seated." She directed them to the couch.

Moments later, a door opened from behind a large desk that sat at the back of the room. Everyone stood up when she entered. She was a very eloquent-looking lady, dressed in a sleek green gown, cut to reveal a modest amount of cleavage. Her coal black hair was tied in a bun with a small rod pushing through the back of it. Bryan could tell this woman obviously was a woman of authority, and well respected.

"Ah! Mr. Ling, and guests," she said, smiling at the men, with a light nod of her head. She offered Mr. Ling her right hand. Mr. Ling took her delicate hand and lightly kissed it. She smiled again approvingly, and sat down in a lounge chair across from the men. "What has brought you here?" she asked.

Mr. Ling immediately answered. "Mama Sandju, we need your assistance. We want to stop some very bad men. Mister Bryan, he explain."

"Ah! Yes, Mr. Wescott." Mama Sandju turned her head to face Bryan. "I understand you saved Mr. Ling's granddaughter from an unfortunate misfortune of enslavement?"

"That's right," Bryan answered. "We were very fortunate to find her. I understand she worked for you, until Lord Baltic had Tony Rema's men kidnap her. She said they were here just before she was kidnapped."

"Yes, Torry worked here for me. She was one of my very favorite employees. I really miss her, as well as several important clients, who also miss her." Her voice rose a bit. "I do hope she decides to return soon." Mama Sandju paused. "You mention Lord Baltic and Tony Rema. You speak of some very bad men," she said, her eyes lifting slightly with the mention of their names.

"Yes," Bryan continued. "We know that Rema is behind several kidnappings in the U. S. As far as we know, at least twenty American women were kidnapped. We have rescued most of them, but there are still a few missing.

"It appears that some very wealthy people pay a lot of money for these hand picked-women. Rema has his men kidnap them, and then transports them to their new owners in, Europe and in the Middle East. We've just learned that at least two Japanese women have also been kidnapped, and we suspect he's behind it."

She listened intently to Bryan's account, and appeared very uneasy with what she was hearing.

"See, Mama Sandju, Colonel Lee Suko is from the North Korean Army and is also involved with Rema. I think you may know him?"

"It's true what you say," she replied. "Tony Rema and his people visit here from time to time, and pay double for each of my employees' services. He also pays me extra to rent my palace for the entire night. Some of my ladies are afraid of him and his men, but they volunteer to service them. They do it because of the money. Rema and his men are very rough on them, and it usually takes two or three days before they can work again."

She hesitated, fumbling with a decision. She knew Rema was a malicious, sadistic man, and his demise might be near. She relented. "What can Mama Sandju do for you, Mr. Wescott?"

"My government has learned that Rema, his ship, and his crew will be just off the coast in a few days. We think they will pay you another visit," he told her.

"You are correct," she replied. "In three days, this Saturday, at four in the afternoon, he has rented my palace for all night. He has paid for ten of my most submissive ladies for his men, but I don't think he will be with them. He has informed me he has other business to attend to.

"If I help you, and turn his men in, he may try to kill Mama Sandju. What do I get in return if I take such a risk?"

"Don't worry," Bryan continued. "That's why Mr. Cane is here. He will coordinate the effort with the local police. You will be protected, and none of your people will be in any danger.

"This is what I can do for you. Mr. Ling has told me you want to expand your business and buy that large empty building next door. I also know the owner has asked more money than you're willing to pay. My government will buy this building for you and provide you enough money to renovate the building any way you want. But we need your help in stopping Rema."

Mama Sandju sat back in her chair and considered what she had just heard. She turned to Mr. Ling. "Can he do what he says?" she asked.

"Yes, Mama, he can do what he says," Mr. Ling replied. "He helped me and co-workers make lots of money in investments. He saved my granddaughter. He can do what he says."

"Okay, Mr. Wescott." Mama's sigh was noticeable. "Here's what I'll do. Rudy will answer the door for Rema's crew to enter the back room. Niki will take each man to a room, and Mr. Cane, your police can take it from there. That's all Mama can do."

Bryan asked, turning to Mr. Cane, "can you work this out?"

"You bet I can. Thank you, Mama Sandju," Mr. Cane replied. He stood up. "I'm leaving right now to set it up. I'll be in touch with you tomorrow." Rudy escorted him downstairs.

"Mr. Wescott," Mama Sandju smiled as she spoke, "Mr. Ling has arranged some entertainment for the two of you. Niki will escort you downstairs to my pleasure palace. Please enjoy.

"Oh! One other thing. Do you know any pretty, young American women that might like to work at Mama Sandju's palace? I can make a lot of money from American women, and they can do as well."

"You know, Mama Sandju," Bryan replied. "I just might know two that might be interested."

"Give these cards to your friends." She signed the backs of two business cards she took from her desk, and handed them to him. "Tell them to return these cards to Rudy. He'll meet them at the front door and bring them to me. You and Mr. Ling go with Niki downstairs, and enjoy the Pleasure Palace."

Mr. Ling and Bryan bowed in respect, and left with Niki. They followed her downstairs to the waiting room and the topless Japanese woman behind the desk. The woman smiled at Niki and typed something into her computer.

Niki waited until she was finished, then said something to her in Japanese. She nodded and looked up at the guard. "Mr. Moto," she said in perfect English. "If you will, please let these three pass." He opened the door and they entered another small hall. Niki stopped at the second door further down the small hallway, lightly knocked on the door, and let them into the private room.

The man inside was young and muscular, and dressed in only a pair of black leather chaps. He stood proudly, his head up and his arms folded in front of him. He was standing beside a young and very beautiful naked oriental woman.

She was restrained to a small table and bent forward at the waist over a rail, attached to the table by two posts. Her knees rested on the table, spread and tied to the same posts. Each of her ankles were tied with ropes, attached to hooks in the floor and on each side of the table. Her position put her ass and pussy up and as wide open as possible. She was ready for full penetration.

Her wrists and arms were behind her back and encircled with several winds of rope with her palms together. The rope that wrapped around her arms pulled her elbows tightly together. Another rope around her wrists was attached to a beam in the ceiling. This pulled her arms up as high as they could go.

Her head was sticking through a hole in a flat board bolted to the front of the table. Around her neck was a black leather collar with four rings, one on the top and bottom, and one on each side. A short piece of rope attached to each ring and then attached to the side of the board. There was no way she could move her head in any direction.

A smaller rope was tied around her long coal black hair and attached to the beam in the ceiling. Bryan figured that was done to keep her hair out of the way of the ring gag that was in her mouth. The gag was securely tied behind her head. He had used the same kind of ring gag himself, and knew the purpose of it.

The three bowed toward the master, and he returned the bow. "Me go first this time," Mr. Ling said. Bryan nodded and moved to the back wall. He and Niki sat down and watched. Niki was a lovely woman in her own right. Bryan would have been plenty happy to just play with Niki, but other things were going on.

Mr. Ling removed his clothes and approached the young master. They bowed to each other. Then the young master handed Mr. Ling a blindfold, and Mr. Ling bowed again. He took the blindfold, and went face to face with the restrained woman. Mr. Ling bowed to her. She could only blink her eyes, as she could not move her head or speak. Mr. Ling then tied the blindfold around her head, covering her eyes.

Bryan was surprised at how much ritual was taking place. It was very unusual; he had never seen anything like it before. So much pomp and circumstance.

Mr. Ling returned to face the young master, and they bowed again to each other. This time, the young master picked up a dazzling colorful towel from a nearby table and handed it to Mr. Ling. He unfolded the towel to reveal a black riding crop with a wide end. The young master stepped to the door and stood there with his arms folded in front of him.

"The master has now given Mr. Ling permission to whip the young girl, by stepping to the door," Niki whispered in Bryan's ear. He heard her soft words, but also felt the wonderful warmth of her breath in his ear. Her body fragrance was intoxicating and mesmerizing.

Slowly at first, Mr. Ling's whip contacted the restrained woman's exposed flesh. Her skin started to turn a light shade of crimson as he continued whipping her. Mr. Ling would periodically stroke his hard cock a few times with his left hand and then strike the woman again as he continued to walk around the table.

Each time the whip made contact, she would shiver from the pain. In her restrained position, it was the only move she could make. Mr. Ling then moved to her backside and positioned his cock directly against her pussy. In a flash, he entered her. She whimpered weakly.

Mr. Ling started to pump forward and then pull almost out. As he pushed forward, he would slap her ass cheek with the whip, and each time she would wiggle from the contact. He was like an artist at work. Each stroke of his whip was planed before it landed.

Bryan watched Mr. Ling closely and was surprised at how long Mr. Ling held back his orgasm. The pumping and whipping never seemed to stop.

Soon, though, Mr. Ling's long-awaited orgasm was getting close. He slowed his action, and then eased his cock from her vagina. Quickly, he moved to her front, and put his cock's head into her mouth. He stroked the shaft a couple more times, then grunted loudly as his seed shot deep against the back of her throat.

When he was through, he moved back to her side and faced the young master. He had now taken the same place by her side as when they had first started. Mr. Ling bowed and presented the whip back to the young master. The master also bowed and accepted the whip. The same procedure was followed with the blindfold.

Mr. Ling joined Bryan and Niki at the back of the room, where Niki handed Mr. Ling a warm wet towel to clean up with. He dressed, and they left after another bow to the young master.

"Your turn now, Mister Bryan. Remember to bow, and wait until the master moves to the door," Mr. Ling said with a smile.

Niki showed the two men to the last room down the hall, and she again lightly knocked on the wooden door. They entered the room like they had done before. The master was older than the first man was. He had a leathery face, with some gray showing on the side of his hairline, but he was dressed the same.

He stood beside another young naked woman, who was suspended by long lengths of rope. The rope was secured to beams in the ceiling and attached to each cuffed wrist and ankle. There was a wide leather belt around her waist with a large ring attached to the back of it, also secured to a sturdy ceiling beam.

The most interesting part was that her arms and legs were in a spread-eagle position. This caused a severe strain on her body. Her body was waist-high and parallel to the floor. Her head was facing down, her long black hair almost touching the floor. Bryan could still see that she was already sporting a big red ball in her mouth, tied very tightly behind her head.

Bryan looked at the master and nodded. The man smiled back and gestured toward the woman, as if to say, "Look what I have for you."

Bryan removed his clothes while Niki and Mr. Ling took a seat against the wall. Bryan then faced the master and bowed like Mr. Ling said he should. The master returned the bow, and then handed Bryan a cat-o'-nine-tales whip. Bryan smiled, took the whip, and again bowed. The master bowed, moved to the door, and folded his arms.

Bryan slowly walked around the young woman and took a closer look at her. She was very young, maybe too young, but he also knew that things were a little different in this country.

He lightly stroked her smooth soft back with the whip's leather thongs, and let the leathery tails slide to the curve of her ass. He repeated the stroke several times, then moved to her upper shoulders and down her back again to her ankles. Bryan's cock had definitely come to life. With each step he made, walking around this lovely woman, it would bobbed up and down like a cork in a pond.

He was teasing her, as if it were foreplay. Her stifled moan was of pleasure and not of pain. He continued his sensual whipping massage. She tried to shift her position in the ropes, but strained as she was, her movements were very limited.

Bryan stopped his sensual whip massage, and with his hands, lightly rubbed her soft, smooth body. She quivered to his passionate touch, her body aflame with desire. She wanted a release and tried to encourage him to take her, but the gag prevented any conversation.

As Bryan continued the massaging to her back and ass cheeks, he glanced toward Niki. Niki's eyes were wide open as she intently watched Bryan's exhibition. He could tell she was almost as excited as the young naked woman, but he knew she had to keep her place. Bryan smiled to himself; she was rubbing her knees together.

Bryan stopped his massage, picked up the whip again, and moved to the woman's back and between her legs. This time, his whip fell against her ass and pussy with tormenting strokes. Scarlet fire raged through her body. "Ugh!" she growled through the gag. Again, the whip found its mark, her body recoiled, and again she growled, "Ugh!" Her hair flew in all directions as she raised and lowered her head.

Time means nothing when a sadist is in session with a submissive slave, and this was no different. Each stroke savagely laced her skin, leaving scarlet lines crossing her tortured flesh. Bryan was usually concerned about the degree of tolerance of a submissive, but this was different. Her body accepted the whipping as if she was some mystical angel, sent from the heavens just to Bryan for his sadistic pleasure. To Bryan, even her moans of agony seemed to have a strange fascination of desire.

He dropped the whip on the floor and started stroking his bobbing cock. Seconds later, he entered the entrance to her open sex. She had already experienced an orgasm, which provided her pussy with enough lubrication to easily accept his massive cock. "Ah! Hum!" she moaned through the gag. She quivered and pulled her head up at his penetration of her open sex.

Bryan grabbed her hair and pulled her head back as far as it would go. He then rammed his glorious cock as deep within her pussy as he could get it. He was in a world of his own now. Never had he had the opportunity to fully explore his sadistic desires to this extent. Even with his beloved Kim, whose nature was so submissive, there was always a limit. He knew Kim would be in for much more—that is, if he could find her.

Soon, his pounding started that familiar tingling sensation in his balls. Most times he could hold his release, but this time, his body took control. He pulled his rock-hard cock out of her steaming hot young pussy. His creamy seed shot across her hot ass and onto her back like a water hose turned on full. "Gah! Damn!" he groaned huskily.

Awkwardly, he stepped back from his conquest and looked up. He caught Niki's eyes again. This time her hand was covering her mouth. She was stunned at what she had just seen. He smiled inwardly again, picked up the whip from the floor, and then moved to stand by the young woman he had just whipped and screwed.

The Japanese master returned to stand in front of him with a knowing smile on his face. Bryan bowed to the man, and he returned the bow. Bryan handed the whip to the master, and again they exchanged bows.

Bryan returned to Niki and Mr. Ling, who were now standing. Niki picked up a warm wet towel like she had done for Mr. Ling, but instead of handing it to Bryan, she went to her knees and toweled his cock for him. She was in no hurry to finish the clean-up task.

Suko's Dungeon (Chapter 10)

"Wake up!" Rema's voice bellowed like a tyrannical male elephant. Kim sat up in bed, awakened from a dreary sleep. He unlocked the chain from the collar around her neck, and after a few minutes in the bathroom, she returned to stand in front of Rema like a stone statue, head facing down and hands by her sides.

"You know your position, now get to it," he commanded, pointing to the table.

She separated her legs and planted them against the legs of the metal table, then put her hands over the table, and lay forward across the top. Rema then tied each of her ankles to the table legs. He finished the process by securing leather cuffs to her wrists and then to the table legs on the other side. Her ass and pussy were now pushed up and opened to make an astonishing target for his whip.

"Can't we miss a day, Rema?" she asked politely, not wanting to agitate him. "You've spanked and whipped my poor ass and pussy and fucked me almost every day since we've been at sea."

"That's right, my dear, I sure have," he replied. He picked up his leather hand paddle and inspected the instrument. "Your man, Bryan, has fucked my operation every day for the last several months. I think this is only fitting. Anyway, you should feel lucky I'm not doing more. Your friend in the next cabin is gonna have a visitor later today. Colonel Suko is flying in and taking ownership of his property. When he gets his sadistic hands on that cute little ass of Janet's, she's gonna be in for one hell of a ride.

"He's gonna stay with us for a few days until we get to his dock and unload our merchandise. He has to get us through North Korean waters—their navy might not like us in their area without him. So he's gonna have plenty of time to amuse himself with his new property. I could give you to him for a session, if you prefer?" he asked.

She had turned her head to listen to what he had been saying to her when she saw his arm rise. The strike came swift and hard. "*No*" she yelled. "*Ahee!*" she screamed at the savage strike. Her body jerked to the tormenting pain of his dastardly paddle. Again and again, strike after strike, the leather paddle landed on her sore scarlet ass. Then Rema stopped the spanking and lightly rubbed the globes of her ass flesh with his open hand. He could feel the heat emanating from her scorched skin. His cock at full erection, he dropped the paddle and inserted his appendage deep inside her waiting canal.

Her nerves were on edge, and her breathing became labored as he pumped away at her defenseless pussy. Her mind raced, wondering how she could continue to handle this madman's continuous intrusion into her body.

Her breasts still hurt from the fishhook piercing to her nipples, but what hurt even more was when he yanked the metal hooks out. Now, her breasts and nipples, still sore, were pressed into the top of the table, and the pain was maddening.

Rema at last finished his savage fuck by shooting his silky cum all over her glorious ass. He slowly backed away from her, admiring her spread body. "You have an amazing cunt, my dear, just amazing," he said. "I know, deep down in that sluttish soul of yours, you love every second of this.

"I'm gonna be on the other ship for most of the day. I'll have one of the crew come in later and feed you. You'd better get used to the position you're in right now. It's gonna be a long day for you," he added.

Rema and Ray were standing at the rail on the *Colletta's* forward deck and talking about the exchange of money and weapons with the North Koreans. In the distance, the low drum of the mammoth seaplane descended from the clouds in front of the ship, and made its approach to land nearby. The seas were calm, and as big a plane as it was, the slight breeze caused it no trouble in landing.

"Ray," Rema suggested, "you'd better put your slut slave into the forward cabin next to mine for the good colonel. He's paid us a great deal of money for her cute sexy little ass."

Suko boarded the ship. "Glad to see you, Colonel," Rema said, putting his hand forward. The men shook hands.

"Good to see you, Rema," the colonel replied.

"Sorry to push things up a bit," Rema said. "We've had some unusual air and sea traffic around. Also, we've found out that our place in Florida has been raided by the feds. I want to get as many guns in the seaplane as possible. The rest we'll take in the sub. Oh! Ray has your new slut slave girl in your cabin. I think you'll be pleased."

"Did she give you much trouble?" the colonel asked, taking his flying headgear off.

The wind whistled across the ship's deck. Rema raised his voice to be heard over the noise. "Ray said she's a real bitch," he replied. "He had to correct some attitude problems, as he called it, but don't worry. I'd never deliver damaged goods." Rema laughed.

"Ha! Ha! Very good, Rema, very good," the colonel replied. "I can't wait to show you my new dungeon. It's a masterpiece. I know you'll love it. She'll be one of many to test all the new equipment. It should be a lot of fun."

Two days later, a cool light breeze blew across a calm blanket of ocean. Rema's submarine of destiny separated from the *Colletta* and started its journey towards North Korea and Suko Point. As the ship neared North Korean waters, Suko radioed the captain of the North Korean Coast Guard patrol submarine. The captain cleared Rema's sub to enter Korean waters and continue to their destination at Suko Point.

Hours later, Rema's sub captain found his way into the small desolate harbor. "Here we are, Rema," Suko said, pointing to the large hangar building next to the water's edge.

"Let your crew have a couple of days off, and enjoy the town. My men will unload the plane and the sub tomorrow," Suko said. "I have your money at my house."

Suko's limo driver stopped the car in front of the main house; the colonel and Janet were the first to get out. Suko unlocked Janet's cuffed hands. "Get on your hands and knees, slave girl," he ordered. She immediately complied with his wishes. He pulled on the chain that was clipped to her collar, and they started toward the front door.

Rema and Kim were the next out of the car, and like Suko, Rema told Kim to get on her hands and knees. "Is this really necessary?" Kim asked desperately. She was completely humiliated by the whole affair.

"Damn right it's necessary. I told you to get on your hands and knees. Do it now, I said."

She knew he meant business, and not wanting to take the chance of making him mad, she complied with his order. He yanked on her collar chain, and they followed the colonel and Janet inside the house. Ray followed a few steps behind the two couples.

The living room was a warm and cozy place for the men to sit and have a drink. Exquisite paintings hung on the walls as if the room was part of a museum. Lavish lounge chairs and expensive carpet adorned the room and the floor. At the marble bar, Ray started to mix drinks for each of the men.

Suko forced Janet to one of the lounge chairs and made her stop in front of the chair. She was in no position to give much resistance. Her body ached from the severe whippings she had endured since Suko arrived on the sub.

Suko sat down in the chair and crossed his feet and ankles over her back. "Ah! That's nice. Mr. Rema, please, take a chair; do the same to your pet. She looks pretty as cushion for feet."

Rema sat down and yanked on Kim's collar. She maintained her balance and took a position in front of his chair, just as Janet had done. Rema sat back and crossed his ankles over her back.

"Mr. Darling," Rema said, "I'm ready for that drink now, and please give the good colonel his. Please make yourself one."

"Mr. Rema," the colonel said. "Me want to thank you for sassy little pet. She's just what me looking for." He took his riding crop and smacked Janet's right ass cheek.

"Aow!" she cried. "Please, sir! *Please!*" her desperate voice whined in the quiet room. "I'll do what you want; please don't whip me any more. I can't take any more."

Suko laughed. "Yes! Yes, I think you're right, pet. I'll save that sexy cunt of yours for later." He laid the whip down on the table next to his chair.

"Mr. Darling," Suko said, pointing toward the bar. "You see briefcase on floor next to the bar? Please put on coffee table and open it." Darling found the leather case and opened it. It was full of American dollars, tied in small bundles.

"Your money, Mr. Rema, as you requested. Four million in cash," Suko said. "My government put a little extra in there for you, as an incentive. They want you to come back and bring more guns, especially those shoulder rocket launchers. After we unload the guns from the sub tomorrow, the money will be yours, and you can even keep the case."

"Thank you, Colonel," Rema replied, "but I do have one question. After we leave, will your navy captain let us pass?"

Colonel Suko laughed. "No worry, Mr. Rema, you're funny," he said. The captain will let you pass. I've instructed him you should call, and let him know who you are. He'll let you continue out to sea."

"Sergeant! Sergeant!" Colonel Suko called toward an adjoining room. A few seconds later, a uniformed man entered the living room, stood at attention, and saluted the colonel.

"Yes, sir, what can I do?" he asked.

"Sergeant, please take our pets downstairs, and lock them each in a cage next to those two Japanese women. We'll be down shortly," Suko said. He took his feet off Janet, yanked on Janet's collar, and made her stand up. He then handed the sergeant the leash. Rema did the same with Kim. They watched as the sergeant led their pets out of the room.

After the men finished two more drinks, Suko said with an evil smile on his face, "Rema, you can count your money later. We need to go downstairs and have a little fun."

They stood just inside the massive dungeon room; Suko turned the chandelier light on. The basement room walls were made of coarse black stone. Rema could feel the temperature change from the living room. Unlike the warm, inviting upstairs, here it was cool, damp, and dreary, just like a good dungeon should be.

He took a few steps into the middle of the room and started to survey the layout of Suko's marvelous new dungeon. Several pieces of expensive bondage furniture were scattered in each corner of the room. There was a spanking bench to his left with a cushioned top and side rails for the slave's knees; it had hooks of all descriptions fastened the on the bench's legs to secure ropes or chains to.

Next to the bench, a few feet away, was a four-foot-tall bondage beam that bolted to a platform and to the floor. The slave would put her cuffed wrists behind her back, and then they could be pulled up and chained to the top of the beam. There was a neck collar chain attached to the base of the beam. This would pull her head almost to the floor, causing her to bend at the waist. Her legs would be spread to each side of the platform and chained to the hooks. This would make an excellent target for an ass and back whipping.

Rema opened the small cage Kim was in and tugged on her collar by the leash. She stepped out, and he made her get back on her hands and knees. "Let's go for a walk, my cherished," he commanded. Rema, with his pet in tow, started his walk around the room, surveying other pieces of exquisitely fabricated bondage and torture furniture.

The crude stretching rack with the large ship's wheel sat in the back of the room. At each end of the rack were leather restraints that attached to some very heavy, thick chains. Kim took a quick glance at the table and was amazed that it so closely resembled the one Bryan had installed in their basement. The only real difference was this ship's wheel was larger.

Rema continued his walking tour, and noticed numerous hooks and rings hanging from large beams that crossed the ceiling; attached to them were huge chains and strong ropes. Each rope was attached to different electric hoists that were secured to beams against the side of the wall.

Rema then stopped at the "X" frame and inspected the device carefully. Attached to the wooden box structure were a series of chains and leather restraints for ankles, thighs, waist, and wrists. He was impressed at the ease at which the frame swiveled. The slave prisoner could be right side up, or upside down, or anywhere in between.

As he and Kim continued their walk, he recognized the two prisoners locked in cages in the back corner of the room. "Suko," Rema looked over his shoulder. "You got two of Mama Sandju's girls in those box cages. Does she know?"

"You know Rudy, don't you?" Suko asked. "When we were there the last time, I asked him if he could come to my house, design, and build me a dungeon in my basement. I think he knows I took those two, but I don't think Mama knows. With the amount of money I paid him, I don't think he's gonna tell her."

Then there was the inconceivable cage. At first glance, it was just another birdcage to keep sex slaves. It stood just to the side of the stretching rack and the other cages. It was like a foreboding evil rock with its own unique portentous structure. After a closer look, there was one remarkable difference. "Would you look at that, Kim," Rema said, pointing to the welded steel construction.

She picked her head up and flipped the hair out of her face. She shivered with horror when she saw it. "I can't believe you'd put somebody in that thing," she said. Just looking at the cage was frightening enough, but to be inside was another ball game.

Arrogantly Rema said, "Get up." He lifted her up by the neck with the chain leash as she tried to stand. The metal door squeaked as he slowly opened the large birdcage. "Be very careful now when you step in; those are razor arrows. If you move around at all, one of those will stick you. The cage is only big enough for you to stand in, and that's about it."

He closed the door and locked it. He was right; the cage was full of arrows welded to the bars, and they were all around her. Any movement of only a few inches, in any direction from her feet to her neck, would cause one of them to sink into her. Some of the arrows were aimed directly at her most sensitive body parts.

"Put your wrists outside the cage," he ordered. He watched her, enjoying the panic in her face. She slowly eased her wrists between the arrows to the cage bars, and then outside. He handcuffed her wrists around the outside of the bars.

The first strike of his whip on her ass caught her off guard. She made a slight instinctive movement in reaction to the sting, but what caused her to scream was the savage pain from one of the arrows in her left breast, just under her nipple.

"*No!*" Her body shivered. She couldn't move. If she did, another one of those arrows would find its mark. "*Damn*! Rema!" she yelled. "You're gonna kill me if you keep this up. Please don't hit me again." The next stroke was even more severe. "*No*!" she screamed again as another arrow jammed into right her breast.

"Silly slut," he laughed. "I can do any damn thing to you I want. I can even beat the living crap out of you, and there ain't a fucking thing you can do about it. You're damn lucky you're such a gorgeous ass; otherwise, that's what I'd do. I'll just leave you like this for the rest of the night. Ha! Ha!" He laughed. "See ya in the fucking morning—that is, if you're still alive." He walked away.

Suko watched Rema's display and nodded approvingly at his efforts. "Rema," he called from across the room. "She's gorgeous, but what about my sexy little minx here? What do you think I should do to her? I've got all this equipment." He gestured toward the main vastness of the room.

"Why not use the rack?" Rema replied.

"Good idea," Suko said. "I've got some other ideas that will work well with that. "Come on, my sassy pet slave," he ordered, yanking on Janet's neck collar. Janet agonizingly looked at him. She knew she was going on an uncontrollable ride of unthinkable horror, and there was nothing she could do about it.

A few seconds later, she lay on the rack on her back. The leather bindings on her wrists and ankles were attached to chains at each end of the rack, almost to her limit.

Suko grabbed the ship's wheel with both hands and turned it a notch, stretching her body almost to her limit.

Click after click, the gear tightened the chains and her restraints. Her body violently pulled rigid, exposing the crossed whip marks on her chest that he had given her the day before on the ship. Her hands turned to fists because of the repulsive strain. She shivered; frightened at the pathetic position she was in.

Her breasts jutted upward, exposing her hard nipples. "If you go *any further*," she yelled, "you'll pull my shoulders out of their sockets! I can't take any *moreee!*" Her yell turned to whimpers.

"Lovely," Rema said. "Just look at those enormous nipples."

"That's a fact," Suko replied. "But you ain't seen anything yet." On the small table next to the rack, he showed Rema a small box. "See this?" he asked. He opened the box to reveal two wire pins, each about four inches long and very thin. He also had a small cork. "Watch this," he said with a wicked smile on his face.

"*No! No!*" Janet yelled again in the silent room. Anguish gripped her face when she saw what he was going to do. "*You can't! Are you crazy?*" Her words fell on deaf ears.

Suko placed the cork on one side of her left nipple, and then guided the razor-sharp pin through the rigid teat until it stuck in the cork. When he finished, half of the pin was jammed through each side of her nipple.

"*AGGGG!*" she groaned. She turned her head from one side to the other, trying to deal with the excruciating pain. Seconds later, he repeated the piercing on her right nipple. "*AGGGG!*" Another frightening groan penetrated the silence.

Sweat started to run down her vermilion cheeks. *"Please, s-s-sir!"* Her nerves and senses were totally out of control. *"I'lllll dooo anything you want, anything,"* she begged. "Please have mercy."

Suko wasn't satisfied. Not yet, anyway. He engaged one of the electric hoists and lowered a rope with a small metal ring attached to it, stopping the rope's movement about a foot from her breasts. "That'll do."

Suko's tied a small string around each pin, on each side of each nipple, and then looped the four pieces of string through the metal ring. Janet's scarlet face struggled with the hot fire that raged through her breasts and nipples. What was this madman gonna do now, she wondered.

Suko had regressed into an animal-like state, only out for the kill, and Janet was his prey. He tied a heavy banana-like weight to the four strings and let it go down slowly. As he let the weight down, her nipples and breasts slowly went upward. Suko stood back, surprised that she didn't scream. Her head had fallen to one side. She had passed out.

Operation Rema's Crew (Chapter 11)

When Bryan returned to his hotel from Mama Sandju's place, several men-dressed in dark business suits were aimlessly standing around. Two were sitting at a table and reading the paper. They appeared to be just everyday guests of the hotel, but he could tell something wasn't right. Call it a gut feeling, but something was wrong.

As he started toward the elevator, his two exquisite stewardesses from the plane walked into the hotel lobby, dressed in matching ravishing scarlet outfits. It was plain to see they were looking for a big mysterious night out on the town. "Ladies," Bryan spoke up in his husky voice, taking a deep breath as he admired their apparel.

"Bryan!" Carmen waved and sashayed her cute little body over to face him. "What's up?" she asked.

"You, and Cindy take these two cards." He handed them the cards that Mama Sandju had given him. "Give them to a guy named Rudy. He'll be at the front door of Mama Sandju's Pleasure Palace. He will take you to Mama Sandju—that is, if you want to experience that spice of life you talked about"

Carmen moved close enough for Bryan to smell her body spray. He cleared his throat. The intoxicating aroma almost released his prize possession from the confines of his shorts.

"Thanks," she giggled like a child that had just been handed candy. "Is this place anything like your room?" she asked.

"Of course," he replied. "You didn't think I'd send you any place else, did ya?"

She took the cards, a glint in her eye. Bryan shook his head as the two stewardesses glided out the front door.

Bryan stepped off the elevator and turned toward his room. There were two more men standing at the end of the hall, arms folded, watching. That uneasy feeling stirred in his stomach again. Something was definitely wrong, but he couldn't put his finger on it. He cautiously entered his room. Bruce Cane and Major James were there waiting for him.

"Those people out there yours?" he asked.

"Yes, Bryan, they are," Bruce answered. Safety first, you know." The tension eased from Bryan's mind. "Oh! Glad you met Carmen and Cindy."

"Carmen and Cindy. They work for us to?"

"That's right, Bryan," Major James broke in. "We had them change their flight schedule to be your backup on the plane, just in case."

"Gee! I didn't know I was that important. Oh, well, what you got?"

"Here's the deal," Major James explained. "We'll pick you up around midday on Saturday. We want to be in place long before Rema's men get there.

"This is what we know so far. The *Colotta* is scheduled tomorrow to anchor about twenty-five miles off the coast and stand by for customs to clear it to dock. Customs has already made contact with the ship's captain, and they're aware we're gonna take the ship. We suspect Rema and his submarine has left the ship and is on the way to North Korea. One of our attack submarines picked up an unidentified submarine signature in the area. One with diesel engines. We told the captain to keep an eye on it, but not to try and stop it."

On Saturday at midday, Bryan sat at Mama Sandju's desk waiting for Rema's men. Only three of Mama Sandju's people were there to help at the door. Rudy would open the door for the men to come inside, one at a time. The topless secretary was sitting at a little desk just inside the door; she would get their names, then Niki would escort each man to another room on the other side of the building. The police would be waiting in the room.

At the prescribed time, the bus arrived at the back of the building, and there came a knock at the door. Rudy opened the door and went out to the bus. He told the crew that because there were so many of them, they would be handled one at a time. As they came in, Niki smiled at each man, took their arms, and led them to the waiting police.

The last man to enter was the ship's captain. Instead of taking him to the police, Niki took him to Mama Sandju's office. Bryan, Bruce Cane, Major James, and three armed guards greeted the captain when he walked in. Rudy followed them inside, shut the door, and stood beside one of the guards.

"Rrrrr! What the hell is the meaning of this?" the captain yelled, his voice coarse and stern. He looked around, and glared intently at the men. Anger pulsated in the veins in his leathery neck.

"Sit down, Captain," Bryan said in a relaxed voice. He gestured toward the chair in front of the desk.

The captain kept glaring at the group of people around him. His stern gaze then turned toward Bryan. "Who the hell are you pirates, and what the Sam hell ya want?"

"No pirates here, Captain. My name is Bryan Wescott," he informed the rebellious captain. "That's Bruce Cane, the U.S. legal representative to Japan. Next to him is Major James. Sit down, Captain, we want to know all about Tony Rema."

Awkwardly, the captain sat down on the front edge of the chair and put his hands on the armrests.

"*Ha!*" He laughed. "Why should I tell you anything about anything? This is an outrage!" he exclaimed. "I've got nothing to say to you pirates."

"Captain," Bryan continued, "I would take another look at things if I were you. I don't think you want to make any foolish choices."

The captain was not easily intimidated. He stared savagely at Bryan, and if looks could kill, the captain would have slashed his throat in a second. The captain knew he wasn't going anywhere for a while, especially with the armed guards standing at the back of the room.

He sat back in the chair and crossed his legs. It was a contest now. "What makes you think I know anything special about Mr. Rema or any of his business? I'm just the captain of the *Colotta*," he said.

"Captain," Bryan began again. "It's like this. We know about Rema's submarine in the belly of your ship. We know about the gunrunning operation and the kidnapped women. That alone is gonna put you and your crew away for a lot of years. At your age, in a Japanese jail, it's a death sentence. They don't like gunrunners, especially when those guns go to North Korea. Yes, we know about Colonel Suko.

"Captain, I'm gonna make you a deal, so you listen up, and think very hard about taking my advice. You answer my questions and tell me all you know about Rema. Our government will intervene and have you and your crew taken back to the States for trial. You and your men will be essential witnesses against Rema. That will get you a lot of time off your sentence. Who knows? You might get out before you die of old age.

"We'll get Rema sooner or later, and this might be your only chance to help yourself and your crew get out of this mess. See, the Japanese will prosecute you and your men for everything Rema has done. You'll take the fall, and he'll be free with the women and all that money. You and your men will be sitting in a Japanese jail for a very long time."

There was a knock at the door. Rudy let the guard in with a message for Major James. "Bryan," Major James broke in. "I've just gotten word that the strike team has taken the *Colotta*. There were only a few men on board. Three of them were injured, one of ours, but no one killed. Rema and the sub are gone as we suspected."

"The captain's expression changed from one of defiance, to one of desperation. The rigid muscles in his face relaxed. "What do you mean, strike team?" He bellowed. "Only a customs inspection was scheduled for my ship. We're supposed to dock tomorrow after the inspection."

"Captain," Major James replied, "the customs inspection was our cover to get the strike team on board. We're just glad no one was killed."

"What do you want to know?" The captain asked turning back to Bryan. Sweat appeared on his forehead. Me and my mates are not gonna take the fall for that sadistic bastard."

"Where's Rema going with that submarine, and who's on it?" Bryan asked. He listened intently for any mention of Kim.

The captain took a deep breath and wiped the sweat from his brow. "Well, he's going to a small point on the southern end of North Korea called Suko Point. I can show you on your map. Rema, Ray Darling, the Colonel, and the two women are on board, along with a crew of eight.

"Those two women have had a pretty rough trip. The second day Suko was on board, he took the one called Janet out to the bow of the ship. To get to the bow, he had to pass by us. We were in the wheelhouse. The woman had streaks of fresh blood on her skin from the whipping he had given her.

When they got to the deck floor, he pulled on a leash that was around her cute neck, and made her get down on her hands and knees and walk to the bow. We could tell Suko had been rough on her. She had a real hard time making her way across the deck.

"He must have whipped her, I don't know how many times. He made her stand at the bow, where he tied her hands to the handrails. The seas were a little rough that day and ocean water was spraying over the edge of the bow. The salt water sprayed her body, causing those cuts to burn like hell. All she did was scream and scream. All Suko did was laugh and whip her some more."

"What about the other woman?" Bryan sat easy, trying to restrain himself. He needed to know all this man knew.

"Oh, the one named Kim? Don't know much about her. Rema kept her chained in the sub and in his cabin most of the time. My men did tell me he would tie her to the table in the middle of the cabin, whip her, and then fuck her. He'd leave her tied like that for most of the day. My men took turns untying her so she could be fed. They would tie her again when they left.

"I did see her come on the main deck one day. She was naked with a metal collar locked around her neck. Rema was leading her around the ship by a leash. He had put clamps on her nipples; a small chain connected the two clips. He had put a heavy weight of some kind on the chain that hung almost to her belly button. I know that must have hurt." The captain paused.

"Mr. Wescott, Rema knows who you are. I heard him mention your name a couple of times."

"Yes, Captain, I've heard that," Bryan replied.

"Suko Point is large enough for the submarine to dock there," the captain continued. "Also, there is a large hangar building over the edge of the water. It houses the seaplane."

"Seaplane?" Bryan responded, surprised at this new development. "What seaplane?" There had never been any reference to any seaplane in Rema's adventures.

The captain explained that Colonel Suko used a seaplane to meet his ship a few hundred miles out at sea. His men had transferred a large portion of the guns from the ship to the plane. The remaining portion of the shipment was in the belly of the submarine.

"Rema told me, that he would be at Suko's house for a couple of days before he returned to meet us. That is, after we unloaded our merchandise on the Japanese dock. I know they were gonna put all the guns in the hangar building until some of the Army personnel could pick them up. At least that was the plan."

"Where's Suko live?"

"I'm not sure, exactly. I've never been there. But I've been told it's about a mile or so down the road from the dock," said the captain. "That's all

I can tell you, Mr. Wescott. Are you still gonna try to help me and my mates?"

Bruce Cane interrupted, "Yes, Captain. I'm the representative to the Japanese government, and we'll start the process right away." The armed guards escorted the captain out the door.

As the men got ready to leave, Rudy called Bryan to his side. "Sir!" he said, a concerned frown on his face. "I know where Colonel Suko's house is."

"How would you know that, Rudy?" Bryan's eyes rose. He was rather perplexed that Rudy would know the answer to that question.

"Sir, about six months ago Rema was here with his men and Colonel Suko. The colonel offered to pay me a great deal of money to come to his house and build a dungeon room in his basement. I spent two weeks working on the project, and I must say, as far as a dungeon is concerned, it's a thing of beauty. Torture there is the word of the day.

"Don't tell Mama Sandju; she doesn't know. I think it's best she not know. Anyway, about two weeks after I returned, two of Mama's ladies were kidnapped. I don't know for sure, but I suspect they're in that dungeon. I'll tell you how to get to his house. Please find these women. They are both very beautiful women, and very helpful to Mama Sandju. One of them is very special to me."

Operation Suko Point (Chapter 12)

"Can you swim, Mr. Wescott?" Major James asked as he continued to pack his equipment bag.

"I guess. It depends on how far," Bryan replied. "I can tread water for a short time."

"I hope so; that's a big ocean out there," the major said with conjecture in his smile.

Bryan could feel the nuclear submarine start to rise from the ocean depths. The pressure in his ears changed. He had felt something similar on the airplane when it took off. Being on a Navy submarine for the first time was definitely an experience. "Where are we now, Major?" he asked.

"About ten miles off the coast, just south of the map position the *Colotta* captain told us. The sub is gonna surface just long enough for the team to deploy our three rafts. It should take us about two hours to get to shore. We use these battery-powered motors; they're quiet but our speed is limited.

"Make sure you wear your night vision glasses; there's not much light but with them you can see. We have to go in under cover of dark," he said.

As the major said, it took the fifteen-man team about two hours to get to the isolated beach that had been designated as the landing point. After hiding the rafts, they made their way over the sandy beach dunes and through some very dense trees. They took a position overlooking the small inlet harbor, and sure enough, there was Rema's sub.

They observed the sub for several minutes before starting down the steep rocky slope that led to deserted road and the dock. They had counted six guards around the sub and the warehouse building next to the side of the dock. They suspected the seaplane was still inside the building, along with all the guns.

Bryan watched as they split into two teams. The lieutenant and his six SEAL team members made their way toward the submarine and dock, while Bryan, the major, and the second group stood by. "Yes, Lieutenant," the major said, speaking into the communications headset. Each man had his own headset radio to talk to the major, if need be.

"Looks like they just filled up the sub with fuel. There's enough fuel for a couple of subs, but a lot of these barrels are empty," the lieutenant reported.

"You know what to do, Lieutenant Harcome. We're going to the house. If you have any problems, let me know." Bryan and the major's group moved down the dirt path that led to the far side of the road. Ten minutes later, they had surrounded the stucco house that Rudy had described. Bryan watched the major's men eliminate one guard after another. Amazingly, they took the men out without making a sound.

Suko, Rema, and Ray were standing in the living room discussing the money, the guns, and the kidnapped women. Suko turned around to see Major James, Bryan, and three strike team members standing at the room's entrance. Each team member's machine gun was pointed toward the men and at the ready. "Who the hell are you?" Suko yelled, enraged at the intrusion.

Suko reached for his handgun, which was lying on the bar, and tried to point it at the men. Major James instinctively pulled the trigger on his machine gun. *Rap! Rap! Rap*! Three shots sped towards Suko and found their mark in his chest. "Ugh!" he groaned and slammed against the bar chair. He clutched his chest as his gun flew out of his hand and across the room. He slammed forward to his knees and fell to the floor. He lay face down, not moving, in a pool of blood.

Ray dove behind the bar and emerged a second later with a handgun. His head appeared and a strike team member fired one shot. *Rap*! The bullet hit Darling just above his nose. A trickle of blood ran down his forehead as the bullet sank deep within his brain. He slammed against the wall behind the bar. His face seemed to stare into oblivious space below the wound; then his body broke several glasses as he fell forward across the bar top. The RANGER team members stood at the ready. They looked at Rema, who was staring in disbelief at what had just happened. His voice was emotionless. "I guess I should just stand here," he said, looking up and turning toward Bryan. "As the late colonel asked, "who are you?"

"I'm Bryan Wescott, and you're Tony Rema, right?" Bryan stepped forward, his machine pistol trained on the man's chest.

"That's right. I'm Tony Rema," he said like a school professor talking to some students. "I know that name. I'm not sure which one of us is more of a son-of-a-bitch. You've killed both Darling brothers and ruined my operation in Greece and London. Then, I got word that you had a hand in destroying my Florida operation, and now this." He laughed.

"I did get some sweet revenge, though," Rema commented with a smirk on his face. "I got that woman of yours. I whipped the hell out of her so many times. She's a great fuck, you know. But I don't guess I need to tell you that now do I?" He chuckled evilly. "She can take the whip real well, and I must say I've had a great deal of fun with her. She's hidden, though, and if you kill me, you'll never find your pussy."

Bryan had been trying to keep his emotions in check, but the hair began standing up on the back of his neck. "You bastard," Bryan replied, starting to lose control. "You're gonna go to jail for the rest of your fucked-up life. I'm gonna see to that!" he exclaimed. "I'll find Kim, and don't think I won't." He shook his gun at Rema.

"Bryan!" the major spoke up, interrupting the confrontation. "They found the women downstairs in Suko's dungeon. Janet, Kim, and the two Japanese women that Rudy told you about. All of them were locked in cages and in rough shape, but they can walk. My guys had to kill a guard down there."

Rema's expression changed; he looked like a man painfully disregarding all the odds against him. "I'm not gonna go to any fucking jail. I may die, but so will you, you bastard." He reached in his coat pocket and pulled out a small handgun.

Rap! *Rap*! *Rap*! Three shots rang out in the silence of the room. The bullets hit Rema in the chest, center mass. A puff of blue smoke filled the air from Bryan's gun as he watched Rema fall forward. Rema rolled over on his back as blood started soaking his shirt.

Bryan stood over the man and faced him on the floor. Rema's face twisted in agony. His voice slurred as he clutched his chest. "*Whoosssseeee heeel ar yaa*? *I'll seess ya in hells*!" Blood started foaming around his purple lips. His eyes started to roll back in his head as he took his last breath.

"I'm just a financial consultant," Bryan replied, staring down at the lifeless body. "I don't think I'll be seeing you again, anywhere."

Almost immediately, a strike team member entered the room with Kim, Janet, and the two Japanese women. "Sir," he reported to the major. "It took us a few minutes to get the women out of those cages, especially the one with the razor arrows. You already know about the guy we shot. Sorry about not having any clothes for the women."

Kim immediately leaped into Bryan's arms and they kissed in a way that electrified both of them. She was breathless and slurring her words. "I's knew you'd comes for meee." She grinned from ear to ear. "I wasn't sure how long it'd be, but I knew you'd come." She continued to squeeze his masculine body, her strength building. Then she looked at Rema lying on the floor, and took a step toward him.

"He's dead, Kim," Bryan said. "He's not gonna hurt you any more, and he won't be kidnapping any more women. Are you okay? I know that bastard was rough on you."

"I closed my eyes," she said, turning back to Bryan. A small gasp escaped her lips. "I pretended it was you. I know that sounds insane, but it was the only way I could get through some of the things he did to me. I'll tell you later."

She again turned away from Bryan and looked at Rema lying on the floor. The unthinkable horror of what had just taken place started to sink in. She walked over to him and kicked him in his balls. After the third kick, and before Bryan stopped her, she reached under his shirt collar and retrieved a set of keys that was around his neck.

Janet stepped away from the ranger who was helping holding her up. She was very weak from the inhuman abuse Suko had inflicted on her, but her mind reeled with delight at the sight of Suko's body lying on the floor in a pool of blood. "Is that son-of-a-bitch dead?" she asked, knowing full well that he was.

"Yes, Janet, he is," Bryan said.

She picked up a whiskey bottle from the bar, opened the top, and took two large swallows. She rubbed her lips with her left hand and replaced the top. She studied the lifeless body on the floor. Without warning, she slammed the bottle into his skull and it broke into a million pieces. The remaining whiskey cascaded over his body.

"Let's go, ladies," Major James said. "We've got a long walk ahead of us, especially with four naked women."

"Bryan!" Kim grabbed his arm. "Why not drive Suko's limo? It's probably still in the garage. That's how he got us here." Major James gave the order for one of his men to check it out.

When they started toward the door, Kim grabbed the briefcase that was on the table beside Rema. She looked at Bryan. "I heard Suko tell Rema there were some important papers about his operation in the case. Maybe it'll help."

A few minutes later, a STRIKE team member stopped the car at the dock next to the hangar. The group met with the SEAL team. "Lieutenant, what's the status?" the major asked.

"Sir, we got all the guards. There was two inside the hangar. It wasn't pretty, but we don't have any injuries. We've wired the hangar building, and we got lucky this time. As far as we can tell, a large amount of weapons are still on the plane. The remaining weapons stash is still on the sub. It's gonna be a big blast.

"We set the radio relay at the top of the hill. When we get out to sea, we can send a signal back and set it off. We're gonna do the sub now; it'll go with the hangar."

"Great," the major replied. "We got the guards at the house and the bastards we were after. The women were downstairs, and we got them out. The house is wired, especially that basement. We have the antenna set; it will all go at the same time the hangar goes."

The SEAL team radio operator rushed into the group. "Sir. I just received word from our sub. Our ride home had to leave to keep from being detected. There's heavy North Korean Navy traffic in the area. Our sub is almost fifty miles out to sea. We can't possibly get to the sub before light. We'd be sitting ducks in the ocean. The sub captain says we may have to hunker down until he can get the sub closer."

"Major," Kim said, overhearing the operator's report. "I heard Suko tell Rema, while they were drinking in the living room, that the Korean Navy sub captain was to let Rema's sub pass. All they needed to do was to make radio contact. They wanted him to come back with more guns. Damn it! Can't your men drive Rema's submarine?"

"You're damn right we can," the lieutenant interrupted. "My men were trained to run an old sub. I'll tell my men not to wire the sub; that's our ride home." The major let out a sigh of relief. "Kim, you're one smart cookie, you know that?"

Two hours later they made contact with the North Korean Navy captain, and when he was told it was Rema's ship, the Koreans let the submarine pass. Later and further out to sea, the lieutenant contacted the American submarine and they escorted the ship to further safety.

"Bryan," Mr. Jeffers said, "that's some story. We saw the large explosion on satellite. You got the dock, hangar, plane, and Suko's house. It looks like this case is closed, or at least this part of it. Nice job, Bryan— Kim, you too. I do hope you're okay. I do have one question, though. What happened to those papers and that briefcase?"

"Mr. Jeffers," Kim said, "when we got out of the car, there was so much confusion; I left the briefcase sitting in the back seat of Suko's limo. The SEAL team wired his car to blow up with the dock and his house. I'm sure the case blew up as well."

"Sir," Bryan said, changing the subject. "What about Kelly and Peggy? Have you heard from them?"

"Yes, we have," Jeffers replied. "They have followed Lord Baltic into a series of caves in the mountains. They said the bandit with him has the last two kidnapped women. It's only a matter of time before they get him."

"There's still two more missing. Ivan Ross is still running loose with two," Bryan reminded him.

"That's correct, Bryan. The Brits said they have a line on Ross, and some safe houses. They're checking on the lead."

"About Rema's sub. What do you plan to do with it now that we have it back in the States?" Bryan asked a glint of an idea in his eyes.

"We're not sure," Greg replied. "Maybe strip it and sell if for scrap. We might use it as a dummy ship for shooting practice. Why? Do you have something in mind?"

"I'd like to turn the ship into a museum at Pikes Point. There's a nice place for it at the marina, and I think people would love to see the inside of a World War II submarine."

"You know, that's not a half-bad idea. I like the idea. Making something positive out of something so negative. I'll set it up."

A month later, Bryan and Kim received a phone call that Lieutenant Harcome and his SEAL team were on the way to Pikes Point. They were driving the sub and would be docking in a short time. Bryan and Kim went down to the dock that had been specially constructed to house the sub.

"Here's your keys, Bryan," the lieutenant said with a smile. "Good luck with the project. I shut the engines down and cut the lights off. Make sure you fasten your seat belt if you take her for a spin," he laughed. With that, he and his crew left in a waiting truck.

"Thanks," Bryan said, waving to the crew.

"Come on," Kim said. "Follow me." Bryan followed her down the small flight of metal steps to the control room of the sub, then down the narrow hall into the main captain's room, where she sat down at the table. "I spent a lot of time chained and tortured on this table. He would let me sleep from time to time, but there were times I was awake, and he thought I was asleep. But I saw where he had several hidden compartments in this cabin. I watched him put stuff in them, and I think you'll be surprised. You see that medicine cabinet over the sink? Look on the side, there's a little latch."

Bryan found the latch and pulled it. The entire cabinet opened from the wall of the sub to reveal a hidden compartment. "What is this?" he said, pulling a briefcase out and laying it on the table.

"Remember those keys I took from around Rema's neck that night? Use this one to open the case," she said.

Bryan's eyes and mouth opened at the same time when he recognized the case. "Damn, you did remember the case that night after all."

He opened the case and was stunned at what he saw. He looked up at Kim but said nothing. "It's a little over four million," Kim said. "Suko said his government put a little extra in there for him to bring back more weapons. There's three more hidden compartments in the cabin. I guess you'll just have to think of something to do to me to get me tell you where they are," she giggled. "It could take some time."

"I'll work on it," he said. "But you're an incredibly beautiful and remarkable woman. I do have some special things I want to try out on you later tonight. Have you ever pulled a cart?"

"Onward and upward." He smiled to himself. "Its gonna be a really great day."

The Saga Continues in "Pirate's Bay"

Follow the works of I. B. Cuffman

In the world of I. B. Cuffman, underworld BDSM fantasies of sexual conquests and sadistic tortures are unveiled in chapter after chapter. His extreme imagination takes his characters on action adventures around the globe.

This is a list of his books, published by Rich B. Publishing for the open-minded sadist.

1. **The Club**: Bryan Wescott is thrust into an investigation to find eighteen kidnapped women. Extremely wealthy people have hand-picked specific women to be their personal property. Gunrunning, sex, violence, BDSM, and torture befall these lovely women.

2. **Pirate's Bay**: Kelly and Peggy, two government agents, rescue two kidnapped women, but wind up in the clutches of a modern-day pirate and his torturous band. Bryan Wescott gets a telephone call to go find them. His destination is an uninhabited island in Pirate's Bay.

3. **Kinkade's Track**: Wade Kinkade is the best tracker in the county. The stagecoach is three days overdue, and the local sheriff makes Wade a deputy. Three lovely women and a lot of money are on that stage. The women are raped and tortured by the bandits that rob the stage. Can Deputy Wade find these women, and what's it all about?

Other books by I. B. Cuffman are in publishing by Rich B. Publishing. For pricing and to order any of these books write to, or e-mail the address listed below.

Rich B. Publishing
P. O. Box 404
Nichols, South Carolina
29581
E-Mail—RichBPublishing@aol.com

Rema's Revenge

www.ingramcontent.com/pod-product-compliance
Lightning Source LLC
Chambersburg PA
CBHW032048150426
43194CB00006B/457